Kello

DATE DUE   9/01

OCT 05 01			
DEC 12 01			
FEB 06 2002			
JAN 03 05			
5-31-05			
JAN 25 06			
GAYLORD			PRINTED IN U.S.A.

waterworks

INVENTING BATH STYLE

BY BARBARA SALLICK

WITH LISA LIGHT

water

CLARKSON POTTER / PUBLISHERS

NEW YORK

works

inventing

bath

style

acknowledgments

The following people brought their own brand of creative production to this project and worked together in the most genuine spirit of cooperation. Each one brought insight and mutual support to the others and all have my special gratitude.

- Peter Sallick optimistically expects that all of our creative endeavors will be both evolutionary and inspirational. Each page of this manuscript was constructed with his unerring and critical eye in mind.
- Lisa Light has been an extraordinary collaborator. Her dedication, diligence, vocabulary, and insight have kept all of the ideas in focus. She patiently tutored me in the "arc" of the book and was there during holidays and weekends to make certain that the content of the book maintained its intellectual and poetic balance.
- Peter Margonelli skillfully focused his lens, clearly seeing the best image in the most fortuitous light to illustrate our point of view. His photographs framed every environment in clear, concise statements.
- J. C. Garcia, our stylist, always used the most minimal intrusions, allowing the fit, proportion, and scale of the spaces to speak for themselves.
- Rick Biedel has made a career of masterfully creating images and drawing memorable lines. Under his direction, this book has been graphically shaped into sleek, fluid passages and balanced visual compositions. At every juncture, we were willing to let his keen eye prevail, as we knew the results would have just the right impact.
- Annetta Hanna and her team at Clarkson Potter allowed us the freedom to write and illustrate a book that spoke clearly to our aesthetic. We thank her for her confidence in our ideas and us.
- And, finally, a special thanks to Robert Sallick, who is my partner, friend, cheerleader, and fellow sleuth. His knowledge of the plumbing industry is encyclopedic. Armed with our mutual interest in design and his knowledge, we have been able to communicate our shared belief that form and function are inseparable.

– Barbara Sallick

Published by
Clarkson Potter/Publishers,
New York, New York.
Member of the
Crown Publishing Group.

Random House, Inc.
New York, Toronto, London,
Sydney, Auckland
www.randomhouse.com

Clarkson N. Potter is a trademark
and Potter and colophon
are registered trademarks of
Random House, Inc.

Printed in China

Design by Rick Biedel / Studio XL, NYC

Library of Congress
Cataloging-in-Publication Data
Sallick, Barbara
Waterworks: inventing bath style
by Barbara Sallick, with Lisa Light
Includes index.
1. Bathrooms – Remodeling.
I. Light, Lisa. II. Title.
TH4816.3.B37 S25 2001747.7'8 – dc21

00-035978

ISBN 0-609-60421-X

10 9 8 7 6 5 4 3 2 1

First Edition

contents

preface

WHEN WE ESTABLISHED WATERWORKS IN 1978,

OUR GOAL WAS TO BRING BETTER DESIGN AND PRODUCT QUALITY TO THE BATHROOM.

WE WERE A DIFFERENT KIND OF SHOWROOM, PROMOTING PLUMBING AS FUNCTIONAL

SCULPTURE, SHOWING ELEMENTS IN REALISTIC INSTALLATIONS, AND GROWING TO INCLUDE

EVERY ARTICLE AND DECORATIVE FEATURE OF THE ROOM IN ONE INTEGRATED PLAN.

TODAY, IN NUMEROUS STORE AND SHOWROOM LOCATIONS AROUND THE COUNTRY, WE

INVITE BOTH TRADESPEOPLE AND CONSUMERS TO FIND EVERYTHING THEY NEED FOR THEIR

BATHROOM PROJECTS, FROM TILES TO TOWELS, FROM ARCHITECTURE TO APOTHECARY.

But at our beginning, the bath was a space being reborn, just awakening to the luxury and variation that the room enjoys now. So we started with the basic equipment: fixtures and fittings, pieces at the core of every bath installation. It wasn't long before we turned to vintage forms and the customs of the European bath for inspiration, and rediscovered the graceful silhouettes, richly worked materials, and handcrafted production that were lacking in American bath designs. These elements had been forfeited with the popularity of molded plastics and trendy, forgettable colors, as the bath became an unwieldy status symbol: who in those days didn't covet the latest shower jet massage or space-age whirlpool, the ultimate sybaritic novelties?

Such indulgences were the most striking rejection of the postwar era of dull bath construction. And though they didn't yet reflect the understated aesthetic we imagined, submerged as they were under layers of brown and orange and acid-green laminate, they certainly embodied a desire for luxury.

Reviving an elegance of design seemed to us an imperative. Looking backward became the basis of something altogether new.

The bathrooms we love today are refined and simple. The archetypal forms are there, but with upgraded engineering, bolder proportions, cleaner profiles. We see artisanal metal finishes, handmade tile, mosaics, stone. Accessories and furnishings now reveal a classic heritage, a deep appreciation of materials and craftsmanship, and an enduring promise of performance.

The bath installation still follows its changeless template: tub, shower, water closet, lavatory; porcelain, metal, tile, stone. (The toilet here is properly called a water closet, the lavatory distinguished from the kitchen sink.) But the design resonates with the glamour of early-twentieth-century industry, as well as the beauty of natural colors and materials and the sensuality of ancient bath traditions. We keep exploring and editing and ultimately expanding on these foundations to create bathrooms that are at once timeless and modern. Add the individual perspective that accompanies each project, and the interpretations of this space grow ever more creative and varied.

With this book we hope to show you examples not just of great bathrooms but also of the fundamental elements and design tools that made them great. Use these pages to exercise your vision and to direct your own design focus toward the myriad small details — the arc of a faucet, the luster of a ceramic glaze, the plush texture of a stack of towels — that make up a lasting bath style.

— Barbara, Robert, and Peter Sallick

water

IT IS ESSENTIAL AMONG ELEMENTS, THE SOURCE OF LIFE. WE DRINK IT; WE COOK WITH IT; WE WASH IN IT; WE HEAL IN IT. THE COMFORTS WATER PROVIDES US FORM A VIRTUAL RECORD OF HUMAN HISTORY – OUR EVOLUTION MIRRORED IN ITS DOMESTICATION, AS WE LEARNED TO TAP SPRINGS AND CATCH RAIN, TO BUILD WELLS AND PLAN AQUEDUCTS. AND BY NO OTHER MEANS HAVE WE SO CELE-BRATED THE BODY, PURIFIED AND PERFUMED AND EXCITED THE SENSES, AS IN THE WATERY RITUALS OF THE BATH.

Not much more than two centuries ago the pleasures of the bath were nearly extinct. Pressurized water was barely imaginable, the ingenious plumbing of ancient Rome all but forgotten. Separate rooms for personal cleansing didn't exist. Bathing took place as a matter of practicality, not delight. Lavatories consisted of a pitcher and basin. Rough, malodorous chamber pots and outhouses preceded the invention of the flushing toilet. And even when the technology of hygiene became available, people were slow to be convinced that they should fit their homes with sanitary "bath-rooms."

Yet today almost every residence has at least one bathroom. What happened? The change reflects a mass cultural shift toward a desire for privacy. The bathroom as we know it is a result of relatively new sensibilities, namely modesty and seclusion – psychological shifts that arose in direct correlation to the development of the modern family home.

As a result, the individual rites of bathing have come to be matters of choice more than requirements of health or social custom. We turn on the water whenever we want it; we can summon it to any room of any building, pump it even to the highest floors of skyscrapers. Innovations of architecture and engineering have thus invited an unprecedented concern with cleanness and well-being.

In the modern bathroom, water remains the central element. It is our conduit to purity, an evocation of nature's pristine abundance, even as we move farther and farther away from its source (in New York City alone, water is pumped from as far away as the Catskill Mountains – a distance of hundreds of miles). It is the vehicle for heat and scent, salt and soap, capable of refreshing with one single droplet or a deluge of suds. Water still energizes when cool, still sweats out impurities when hot. It is still steam, vapor, soak, and balm.

And water is always a momentary visitor. Its arrivals and departures are determined by far more permanent equipment; structures at once sensuous and inviolable, pervaded by water and yet immune to it. In the bathroom, water penetrates only skin. For this purpose we have lured it indoors, to lay ourselves bare in its wake. But as tamed in here as it will ever be, the water still flows with tantalizing abandon. In the private room that we've built up around it, it still frees us to do the same.

part I

habitat

HERE ARE THE UNCHANGING RULES OF THE BATHROOM: THE MAJOR FURNISHINGS ARE CONSTANTS; THE CORE MATERIALS ARE ALL HARD. THERE'S NO GIVE AGAINST THE SLICK SURFACE OF A TILE FLOOR, THE INFLEXIBLE SCULPTURE OF PIPES AND PLUMBING, THE EXACTING SLOPE OF A TUB WALL. SUCH OUTFITTING CREATES A REAL SENSE OF PERMANENCE: UNLIKE MOST OTHER ROOMS IN THE HOME, WHERE ELEMENTS CAN BE MOVED AROUND AT WILL, REFINISHED OR RECOVERED, BATHROOMS STAY THE WAY THEY'RE BUILT. AND THEY'RE MEANT TO LAST THAT WAY FOR A LIFETIME.

This is a space where every vital feature is in some way anchored to a wall or floor, where the entire installation must perform under unique conditions of humidity and water, where equipment is presented as furniture. It's a puzzle of hardware, a cold white box.

Add to this the concentrated way in which people interact with the room – the proximity of face to mirror, the intimate splash of water against skin, the bare feet, the exposed fixtures. No matter what size the space itself is, the bathroom is a place of close-ups. There's something vulnerable about that *nearness,* about the extreme contact of getting clean.

In a room like this, where there are no buffers, where we feel each surface so directly, psychic comfort and safety are critical. Here an attention to detail and craftsmanship becomes essential. Every part of the hard blueprint should stimulate the senses, even before a single transitional element – textiles, accessories, apothecary goods – enters to soften the experience.

Fleshing out the bathroom's shell starts with investing in the practical furniture the room has to hold: selecting fittings and fixtures that show an elegance of line, covering walls and floors with sensuous materials. It means energizing the relationships between all the fixed elements in order to create a vivid space. These details will transform the cold white box into a humane habitat, rich in design and efficient in operation.

design

integrity

DESIGN INTEGRITY DEPENDS ON GOOD CRAFTSMANSHIP. IN THE BATH-
ROOM IT MEANS THAT HARDWORKING EQUIPMENT SHOULD BE BUILT TO
LAST AND THAT EACH FURNISHING SHOULD BE PLEASING TO THE TOUCH
AND THE EYE. DESIGN INTEGRITY PROMISES THAT FINISHED QUALITY MAKES
A DIFFERENCE AND THAT CLASSIC COLORS AND MATERIALS WILL BE MORE
REWARDING THAN TRENDY ONES. LIKE ANY OTHER DECOR, THE EMPHASIS
IN THE BATHROOM SHOULD BE ON ENDURING STYLE.

Design integrity demands a focus on the parts that make up the whole – the uniqueness of every stone in a floor, the precision construction of a showerhead, the crisp installation of grout and tile. Just as a good car or a well-built house is marked by a balance of engineering and art, the bathroom should be the sum of its many details. Elegant design and refined craftsmanship in every component will give the overall space a heightened – and lasting – look of luxury.

decoration

GOOD DECORATION AIMS FOR AN ESSENTIAL HARMONY IN WHICH THINGS FIT TOGETHER. IT'S A MATTER OF CHOOSING THE RIGHT INGREDIENTS AND ASSEMBLING THEM WITH CLARITY AND STYLE. IT STARTS WITH THE FIXED ELEMENTS OF AN INSTALLATION, THEN INTRODUCES SUPPLEMENTAL ITEMS (TOWELS, ACCESSORIES, FURNISHINGS) IN A LOGICAL AND PLEASING RHYTHM. TO ENSURE THE INTEGRITY OF THE VISION, EACH ELEMENT SHOULD BE PART OF AN OVERALL DESIGN.

Decorating is about individual sensibility and selection. There is no one formula for good design, and no particular decorative style surpasses any other in the fleshing out of a raw space. Rather, decoration is about committing to an aesthetic in details large and small, choosing different motifs of color, pattern, and form, and making sure, in both the space and its furnishings, to get the bones right, through attention to graceful proportions. The subsequent placement and interaction of elements will produce a chemistry that fuels the total space, instead of relying on set dressing to enliven a passive background.

Every material used in the bathroom should be decorative and should have its own beauty. When combined in a thoughtful way, these materials will result in a room that looks richly integrated. Marble next to metal. Mosaic beneath ceramic. Intricate pattern against smooth expanse. A layering of colors and textures. The contrasts between adjacent elements will create dynamics and rhythm, binding the hard and soft layers of the space into a fully rounded environment.

luxury

EXTRAVAGANCE IS NOT THE SAME THING AS LUXURY. TRUE LUXURY

IS A RICHNESS OF MATERIAL AND CRAFT, A WISE AND COMFORTABLE USE

OF SPACE, A SPIRIT OF DECORATION. IT IS THE PRACTICE OF SENSUOUS

RESTRAINT, WHERE A SELECTIVE USE OF DESIGN ELEMENTS CAN OFTEN

PROVE THAT LESS IS MORE.

Luxury resides in the details, and in a knowledge of good design that allows those details to breathe. Constraints of square footage are no liability: precise placement and integrity in individual furnishings will always speak of quality. A small bathroom, then, can be just as luxurious as a large one.

A deeper understanding of luxury comes from education. It's learning why a handmade piece is better than a mass-produced one, because of its greater sensory appeal, its longer life, its superior performance; an understanding also of why different elements combined in a certain way evoke a feeling of comfort: furnishings scaled and arranged to meet the needs of a personal routine. And why a crisp installation is as important as the materials that go into it: tile settings and spatial proportions that preserve the balance of the overall space.

Such concerns produce a bath interior that is transparent in operation, where the senses are directly engaged by the quality of service: the pulsing morning shower, the bathtub's soothing depths, towels at the ready, clutter concealed, mirror well lit and flattering.

A luxurious bathroom can reflect any style, but it will always make room for the simplest bodily pleasures, the warmth and water and fragrances that take time to unfold – the ultimate luxury in an age of speed.

part 2

essentials

THE BATHROOM CONTAINS APPARATUS BUILT TO HOLD, HEAT, MIX, DRAIN, FILTER, AND DEFLECT WATER. THESE ELEMENTS FUNCTION AS AN INTERFACE FOR A BUILDING'S STRUCTURAL PLUMBING, A NETWORK OF PIPES LAID INTO THE RAW FRAMEWORK AND REACHING OUTSIDE TO MAIN WATERLINES. THIS SYSTEM IS UNIQUE: WHILE OTHER HOUSEHOLD EQUIPMENT IS NOT DEFINED BY ITS JUNCTION WITH THE UNDERLYING POWER GRID – THE PLUG OR CORD, FOR EXAMPLE, IS NOT PART OF A REFRIGERATOR'S OVERT DESIGN – THE BATH'S APPARATUS MUST EMBODY ITS SOURCE.

Faced with that necessity — that pipes have to be tapped, that water needs to turn on and off and be carried away — the mechanics of bath design are indivisible from their aesthetics. Nowhere else in the interior does form so closely equal function.

There is a fundamental logic to each design in this landscape that explains its operation: nonporous glazed porcelain for basins and water closets because the surface does not absorb bacteria and because it is smooth and integral and won't catch dirt in seams. Tubs and lavatories adapted from classical freestanding shapes because those forms best accommodate the body's natural curves. The arching pipe as faucet, moving water with the simple anatomy of an artery; taps and handles that turn in the hand like a key in an ignition, allowing control of the plumbing engine; a perforated showerhead to spread one channel of water over a wide surface. All show a technology of containment and release of water that has changed little over thousands of years.

The items that make up this apparatus are classified into three main categories: fixtures, fittings, and surfaces. Every installation begins with some combination of this trio, a convergence of the materials used to transmit water and the fixtures designed to hold it.

At their best, the workings of each piece will be revealed rather than concealed. The emphasis is on a balance of presentation and performance, so that function is never subordinate to facade.

fixtures

FIXTURES ARE THE BATHROOM'S PERMANENT FURNITURE: TUBS, LAVATORIES, WATER CLOSETS, BIDETS. THESE ELEMENTS ARE ALL IN SOME CAPACITY CONTAINERS FOR THE BODY, SO THEIR PROPORTIONS ARE PARAMOUNT. A LAVATORY MUST NOT BE TOO DEEP OR TOO SHALLOW; THE HEIGHT OF COUNTERS SHOULD BE COMFORTABLE; A TUB SHOULD BE LONG ENOUGH FOR THE BODY TO STRETCH OUT IN.

Wherever the space allows, it is preferable to choose fixtures that perform independently – separating the bath from the shower stall, for example, or adding a second lavatory in a bathroom used by several people. Fixtures with just one purpose tend to have cleaner lines and a more advanced operation than those with dual responsibilities.

In terms of design, fixtures are the most universal items in the bathroom. The characteristic that most often anchors them is color. White is the standard for all these components, and it is always a flawless choice. Metal and marble also work well here. These materials have their own history in the bath, and they provide an interesting counterpoint to the room's traditional white terrain.

lavatories

FOR EACH FIXTURE, VARIATIONS IN STYLE ARE AMPLE.

Lavatories alone come in a dizzying range of designs and silhouettes, yet all are derived from the basic composition of basin, stand, and faucet. Choices range from freestanding pedestals to cabinets, consoles, and wall-mounted models; from clean-lined washstands to revival wash tables; from organic curves to geometric platforms. They can be fabricated in simple porcelain or in mixed materials including wood, marble, metal, and glass. Basins can be round, oval, or rectangular; they can be sunk into a surrounding deck or raised above it like fonts. Silhouettes can be sculptural or architectural, airy or massive.

All these choices have a different impact on a site that hosts the most varied and frequent stops in the bath routine, from washing the hands and face to brushing the teeth and shaving; from applying makeup to bathing a baby. Add to this range the flexibility of the format in terms of the space it consumes: the lavatory can shrink to fill a small space or expand to balance out a large one. Of all the bathroom's fixtures, the lavatory is most flexible, capable of meeting the diverse needs of its users and the space it has to occupy, for which it must be more adaptable in scale and mass than any other form. Other fixtures are obliged to be big enough to hold the whole body; the lavatory needs room only for a pair of hands.

This vintage pedestal lavatory features a comfortable, deep bowl and an unusually wide lip, allowing space for essential accessories around the basin. The architectural base offsets the undulating mass of the deck, keeping the profile from looking overly heavy.

In surveying the numerous styles available for the bathroom lavatory, keep in mind a few important specifications. These relate to the depth, diameter, and standing height of the basin.

Lavatory bowls should be at least 6 inches deep to prevent water from splashing onto counters or floors. If the basin is any shallower, water will splash over the rim when you wash your hands, and the running stream from the faucet will spray over the sides. Conversely, a much deeper basin may in fact be too deep for comfort unless the lavatory is often used for laundry and infant bathing. In a multipurpose or loft-like space where the lavatory is expected to play such a domestic role, you can use a flat-bottomed farmhouse or kitchen sink. Most modern lavatories, however, are used for running, as opposed to still, water. For this reason, lavatory bowls have evolved with rounded sides and bottoms to help channel the flow of water into the drain.

Because bowl shape varies so much, diameter is also variable. In a high-traffic bath, look for a basin that is no less than 19 to 20 inches wide, 15 to 16 inches from front to back, and 6 inches deep. In a powder room where the lavatory is used primarily for washing hands, the basin can be narrower but no shallower and no shorter from front to back in order to prevent splashing.

As people have grown larger and taller over the last century, the lavatory's height has risen commensurately. Traditional and vintage lavatories place the basin at 31 inches high; today, however, it is more common to see a height of 33 to 36 inches. Your chief goal in specifying height is to reduce back and muscle strain caused by stooping and bending.

Certain lavatories, including wall-mounts and consoles, can be installed at a custom height, as can metal frame washstands. These are the best choices for people who are shorter or taller than average. Molded porcelain fixtures and wood-frame wash tables and vanities are usually manufactured at industry standard heights.

In all these dimensions, fit with the body is essential to the performance of the fixture. The best way to check the fit is to try out different lavatories in the showroom: stand in front of each model, bend over the basin, relax, and lower your hands into the bowl. As much as you might favor the vintage pedestal base for its look, if the lavatory does not suit your height and posture, it's not the right choice for your bathroom. It will be awkward to use, detracting from the comfort that is so much a part of a luxurious bath experience.

How a lavatory basin meets its base classifies the format of the overall fixture. The lavatory can be molded as a continuous unit with its deck, as in traditional porcelain forms, or it can be independent — a basin dropped into a counter. This latter version opens up the design of the fixture to a wider range of materials, including metal, glass, stone, and earthenware.

Combination lavatory-counters may sit as independent pieces atop a pedestal or washstand base, or they may be wall-mounted. If the mount is supported by a base with front legs, the fixture is called a *console*. Whether angular or curvilinear, porcelain consoles usually have smooth bowl lines with softened edges, a result of the ceramic fabrication and its seamless glaze. They are also the most familiar lavatories, having dominated bathroom decor from the early 1900s through the postwar era.

The lavatory in a *deck mount* may be installed in any of three ways: set directly on the countertop, dropped in, or under mounted for a sleeker profile. All three styles can be used in conjunction with open consoles or closed vanities, and they all typically feature counters made of a slab material like wood or stone.

In *drop-in installations,* the rim of the bowl sits up on the counter, usually fixed in place with silicon. This rim creates a frame in the counter and is especially attractive when the bowl is fashioned of a high-definition material like hammered nickel or copper. In *under-mounted installations,* by contrast, the bowl is affixed to the underside of the counter with silicon and clips. This method produces the cleanest edge where the counter material itself creates the rim, allowing water to be wiped directly into the bowl.

Any vessel with a conventional drain opening can also be plumbed in a *wash-table format.* Innovative elements include vintage bowls and sculpted stone urns, turning the original lavatory format into a modern design option. The relatively new use of the *washstand* — most commonly a three-sided metal base with an under-mounted basin and marble top — is another reinterpretation of bath history, drawing on a style from the early 1900s. Slimmed down and given smooth, unadorned legs, but preserving the luxury of a stone countertop, the washstand produces a streamlined architectural look in keeping with the appreciation for Art Deco and industrial themes in design today. Other elements, including traditional porcelain decks in combination with metal frames, as well as milled wood counters or bases, can also create a washstand profile with an architectural effect.

Closed vanities first appeared in the late 1880s; but they came to prominence in the postwar era, reflecting the need for increased storage in baby boom homes. Today these fixtures can suggest a wide range of interior styles, from modern to rustic to Colonial. This use of cabinetry offers a good way to bring the warming texture of wood into the bath. For a cooler direction, custom stainless-steel cabinets, inspired by midcentury medical and office equipment, are a popular choice.

In any type of lavatory, whether console or vanity, pedestal, washstand, or wash table, the choice of material sets the mood as much as the silhouette does. Porcelain is timeless and classic in white and promises to remain pristine. A white Carrara marble sink or countertop is a marvelous luxury. Marble and other types of stone may stain, however, so choose this material only if you like its irregularity and changing patina. (Because of stone's staining potential, we don't recommend its use for lavatories in children's bathrooms.)

New types of molded glass for basins and counters offer a very modern look with an intriguing element of transparency, and work beautifully with metal washstand frames. Nickel and copper basins combine elegantly with darker marble and wood decks. These metals can deliver a glamorous effect when buffed to a smooth finish, or they can produce a vintage feel when left hammered and weathered. A hammered texture that is brilliantly polished produces a third look that can work beautifully with a matte-finished countertop.

bathtubs

it is even more so for the success of a bathtub. Like any garment or pair of shoes, the bathtub is a vessel that must be tried on to fit the contours, angles, and length of the body; accordingly, the fixture comes in varied shapes and sizes to accommodate different body types. Purists can select a freestanding cast-iron tub, with classic claw feet, for example, or a Roman-inspired urn shape on an oval base. A number of modern skirted models are also available, in which the exterior of the bathtub is concealed by an apron. Deck installation is another alternative. This format can be clad in tile or stone, or paneled to suggest fine furniture. In addition, a deck can conceal the circuitry and pumps of your whirlpool system.

Ovals, rectangles, ellipses, and radius-ended silhouettes are the most traditional bathtub shapes, though with moldable acrylic, many shapes are possible, including corner tubs and the heart-shaped models that are synonymous with honeymoon kitsch. Bathtubs may have a slope on one or both ends, creating a single or double orientation. Shape is further affected by the placement of the tub filler. The plumbing may be centrally positioned to accommodate a double-curved interior, or it can be installed on the drain end of a single-sloped tub.

A freestanding claw-foot tub takes on a practical double role with the addition of an overhead shower. The vintage-style exposed plumbing and perimeter curtain hoop echo the exposed silhouette of the fixture.

While tub silhouettes have remained relatively constant, dimensions in the last half-century have begun to change, dramatically improving the comfort of the bathtub. Beginning in the prewar period, when the form was first standardized, bathtubs were available in a variety of lengths, including 4½, 5, and 6 feet, but they were very narrow. After 1945, the 5-foot by 30-inch by 14-inch skirted profile became the norm in the new 5-foot by 7-foot bathrooms. This size was purely a result of mass production, and it added to the very homogeneous look of bathrooms in the decades that followed World War II.

Today the standard tub size has increased to 5½ feet by 32 inches. Stock sizes have also begun to vary as manufacturers recognize that consumers are taller and larger, and are interested in bathing as a leisure activity. Common dimensions to look for include 5 feet by 33 inches, ideal for children and vintage-scale rooms; 5½ feet by 34 inches; 6 feet by 36 inches; and, for double occupancy tubs or large-size adults, 6 feet 6 inches by 39 inches. Bathtubs of regular depth measure from 14 to 16 inches, while soaking tubs add several generous inches to top off at 20 to 21 inches.

These larger proportions make all the difference between function and luxury in this fixture. The goal in tub bathing is to be able to slip under the surface of the water so that your shoulders are covered – without displacing floods of water over the rim. If your shoulders or your bent knees must be exposed to the air for the rest of your torso to be submerged, then your body will chill and periodically need to shift position in order to stay warm. A sensual tub experience edits out this disruption by making sure there is enough room for the body to submerge comfortably and completely.

With so many models available, it is vital to test different tubs and compare them for comfort and volume. Go to a showroom and work with an experienced design consultant. Ask about tub sizes or shapes you may not see on the sales floor. Consider the advantages of a freestanding form versus the potential for specialty features, such as whirlpools, in a deck installation. Evaluate your need for surrounding counter space; look at decks clad in different materials. There is truly no way to evaluate this fixture in a blueprint or in a catalog photograph. As in buying a mattress, much of tub selection is about actually "trying" the tub, to appraise its legitimate fit as well as to satisfy stylistic preference.

An enclosed overmount tub is framed by peripheral deck space for balance in proportion as well as accessible placement of bath products. The tile cladding follows the wainscoted walls, minimizing the frontal mass of the fixture in this small room.

Choice of materials is important in selecting a tub. For most of the modern era, cast iron has been the material of choice for bathtub fabrication. Not until the early 1980s was acrylic considered a truly viable alternative in America, though it had been used in England and Australia since the late 1940s.

Today's acrylic offers benefits that are unattainable in cast iron, making it in many ways a better material for tubs. This may come as a surprise to anyone who remembers the flimsy gel-coated "fiberglass" bathtubs of the 1970s and 1980s. Not true acrylics, those forms were by all counts insubstantial, and inspired a list of complaints that eventually made the fabrication obsolete: they warped, were noisy, scratched easily, faded in ultraviolet light, and virtually soaked up dirt.

What they did do, however, was permit the introduction of whirlpool systems and molded deck installations in a variety of shapes and sizes, assets to which the new acrylics are heir. In a room where natural materials are recommended for their imperfections, texture, and warmth, this is one area where technology has improved on nature, producing a plastic with greater longevity and flexibility than any organic medium suitable for tub design.

Modern acrylic bathtubs are extremely durable and sanitary, and deliver a perfectly smooth, blemish-free surface as well as superior integrity of fit. The material has a radiant luster that is compatible with the porcelain used for lavatories and water closets. And it is nonporous, making it resistant to staining from impurities in water and thus easier to clean.

Because hygiene is so important, the majority of acrylic bathtubs contain an antibacterial agent called Microband, which inhibits the discoloration and filmy residue caused by surface molds and mildew. This is an integral ingredient blended homogeneously through the acrylic sheet, rather than a sealant or coating applied on the surface. As a result, it is present for the life of the tub, helping to preserve a bright, new-looking finish over many years.

Acrylic is also energy-efficient. It is naturally warm to the touch and so does not need to draw heat out of the bathwater. As a result, the only real heat loss in an acrylic tub comes off the surface of the water. Cast iron is a comparatively cold material that takes a longer time and a greater amount of hot water to warm up; it also continually absorbs heat out of the water into the sides and bottom of the tub. Acrylic is more slip-resistant, too, and so does not require a textured bottom to enhance traction.

Acrylic bathtubs can be molded in a smooth, continuous shell, or they can be fitted with a whirlpool system. Bringing this material full circle, new freestanding forms are currently being developed by a number of manufacturers that will incorporate all the benefits of acrylic into the most traditional bath designs.

When choosing an acrylic bathtub, inquire about the addition of Microband, and make sure to ask about the thickness of both the acrylic sheet and the backing fiberglass. The backing is what gives the fixture its sturdiness and strength as well as help with insulation; for major sanitary products like tubs, the better manufacturers provide fiberglass that is $\frac{3}{8}$ inch to $\frac{1}{2}$ inch thick.

High-quality acrylics should have a seamless finish, so imperfections, pits, and a wavy or textured tub bottom are typically indications of a thin acrylic sheet. The shell should also sit perfectly flush with the deck, whereas cast-iron shells will often have a bow, requiring filler to seal the tub edge to the deck. Looking for this fit is one way to differentiate between the two materials. In addition, cast iron in a certain light will show a rippled or mottled texture, commonly known as orange peel. Acrylic should be perfectly flat and smooth by comparison, a benefit that makes reclining on this surface a more pleasant tactile experience.

Despite the vast improvement in acrylics, many people still prefer *cast iron* and other traditional materials such as copper, marble, and ceramic. Cast iron is substantial and durable, and to date it is still the prevailing material for freestanding tubs. A few classic cast-iron styles remain in production; new styles will be similar in texture and silhouette to vintage pieces. With hard-to-find older models whose enamel has begun to wear down, you should pursue re-enameling with caution: the name of this service can be misleading, as the coating will actually be baked-on epoxy paint. True enameling requires surface stripping and high temperature refiring, so the tub has to be removed from its surroundings.

Old fireclay tubs – the first modern tubs – surface periodically at antique fairs. These tubs, dating from the mid- to late 1800s, are surprisingly large, but they're extremely heavy; a typical example may weigh in at 800 to 900 pounds. In their own time they were expensive and difficult to produce – drawbacks that ultimately led to the rise of cast iron, a lighter weight and more affordable material. Yet for elegance of line and lustrous ceramic tone, the early fireclay tubs are matchless. If you find one in good condition, make it the centerpiece of your installation.

Copper tubs, which derive largely from French tradition, hit their prime in the late nineteenth century. A few manufacturers in Europe still make them today. These freestanding units have an elemental, rustic appeal and tend to possess high sides for a deep water fill. All tubs of this nature should be tinned on the inside to prevent copper from leeching into the water. From a design perspective, the use of two metals adds to the visual appeal of the form.

Marble in all its applications is elegant, but in the crafting of tubs it is a difficult material to master. Custom tubs made of marble slabs can exhibit modern, almost Japanese-looking lines; some designers have incorporated slanted backrests into the form to give the fixture the look of an oversize recliner. When using marble slabs, however, be aware that corner seams can catch dirt and bacteria. The stone also has a very cold surface that is difficult to heat; like cast iron, marble will draw warmth out of the bathwater. A better way to introduce marble into the tub setting is as cladding for a deck platform. Here it will make a prominent statement while leaving the fabrication of the tub to more appropriate, seamless materials.

The development of the whirlpool is perhaps the most prominent event in the rebirth of domestic bath luxury. Patented in 1966 under the trade name Jacuzzi, this system for home tubs brought a therapeutic advantage to the bath that had previously been available only in spas and hospitals. Once the whirlpool was embraced by private users, other amenities and breakthroughs followed, reinstating a focus on wellness and pampering that the bath hadn't seen since the 1920s.

The whirlpool was and is primarily a rehabilitative device that provides hydrotherapy – the use of water massage to loosen muscles and stimulate circulation. The system works by pulling water in from the tub, mixing it with air drawn in from the atmosphere, and distributing it out a series of jets in the form of bubbles. When the bubbles hit the surface of the body, they explode, creating a micromassaging action. Combining this action with hot water raises the blood flow and relaxes the muscles.

The most important thing to consider in any whirlpool system is what kind of massage you want. Only where the jets hit the body will there be massaging action, so if you wish for a back massage, for example, you should select a model with jets at your back. Foot massage requires jets at the foot end of the tub; leg and calf massage places jets low on the sides of the fixture.

Before you select your whirlpool system, sit down in the shell and test the environment. Notice where the jets on different models are placed, as well as how they're angled, to make sure the bubbles hit your body in the desired spot. Many systems run today on internal censors that eliminate the need for unsightly switches anywhere on the face of the fixture, so the interface is in a real way reduced to the placement and symmetry of the jets.

In terms of operation, dual suction fittings are valuable. This feature helps the system in two ways: it makes the pump more efficient, and the second suction acts as a relief valve, should a bather come in contact with the fitting. This latter trait makes the whirlpool safer, particularly for small children: a single suction can pull a child down like an undertow, and it can trap girls with long hair and drag them underwater. Even with dual suction, the equipment can be dangerous; under no circumstances should a child use the whirlpool unsupervised.

Over the long term, the performance and safety of a whirlpool is wholly reliant on maintenance. Water left in the system's pipes can be a breeding ground for bacteria, so it is absolutely essential to your well-being to disinfect the mechanicals of your whirlpool bath regularly with special cleaners. Otherwise, when you turn the system on, you run the risk that bacteria will enter the tub and pollute the fresh water. Cleaning should be done on a monthly basis at least – or more frequently depending on how often you use the system.

water closets

This fixture represents a triumph of sanitary engineering, late though it is in the history of bath design: its fundamental conception is so ideal that little has changed in its workings or silhouette since its adoption in the 1880s.

Invented in 1596 by Sir John Harington, this vital piece of equipment did not catch on until almost two hundred years later when, in 1775, the first flushing water closet was manufactured in England. Another hundred years passed before the fixture advanced to its current state, having been refined and standardized by English designers such as George Jennings, Edward Humpherson, and Thomas Crapper, who foresaw the plumbed latrine as an implement essential to public health. It is astonishing to consider that after millennia of chamber pots, cisterns, and outhouses, the water closet is a convenience barely out of its first century.

Some water closets may be installed without a tank, freeing up both visual and physical space along the wall. If you do have a tank, take advantage of the ledge for a display that will soften and humanize the fixture.

54

and bidets

In silhouette the modern water closet is basically a streamlined version of its early English predecessors. Along with the companion bidet – a sitting basin fitted with a water jet to bathe the perineal area – varied models look much alike from the frontal view, but in profile, tanks and bases will show subtle differences. Shapes can be elongated or compact, contoured or geometric, Georgian or Palladian. Look for forms with an augmented bowl length for a more comfortable and supportive seat; these designs also move the body forward on the fixture, creating extra clearance from the wall. Lids and seats of finely milled beech or mahogany, molded plastic, or painted wood composition add further design options.

Technically, the performance of the water closet depends on the quality of the valves in the tank and the design of the trap in the bowl. Federal energy conservation laws dictate that a tank can use no more than 1.6 gallons of water for flushing, a quantity far reduced from the 3.5 gallons previously accepted. Newer systems compensate for this deficit in water pressure a great deal better than the older models.

Notwithstanding the lower water level, the workings of this fixture can and should be swift, clean, and continuous. Select a unit from a maker with a reputation for good engineering to ensure a quick, powerful flush and a fast but quiet fill.

If you care to have a bidet, choose a model from the same design group as your water closet, so that the forms make a coherent suite. While this secondary fixture is still more common in Europe than in America, most well-known manufacturers and distributors do offer bidets that coordinate with classic water closet designs.

fittings

FITTINGS ARE THE BATHROOM'S HARDWARE AND VISIBLE PLUMBING.

THEY INCLUDE FAUCETS, SPOUTS, AND HANDLES; SHOWER SYSTEMS,

TUB FILLERS; MIXERS, DRAINS, AND VALVES – EVERY DEVICE THAT

DELIVERS OR DRAINS WATER TO OR FROM A FIXTURE.

These pieces are the most industrial elements of a bath installation, in that they are virtually always a formal extension of the plumbing system in the wall. Yet pull any faucet out of its deck and its working components – the pipes that hook up to the plumbing channel – are in their own rough way as well-fashioned as anything above the surface. The difference lies in the added articulation of detail and in the skillful finishing of the surface metal. This is where fittings acquire their particular quality, like a stone faceted and buffed to a gem. Punctuating the bare planes of fixtures, they become the bathroom's jewelry, as finely shaped and polished as any ornament.

Plumbed fittings exemplify the modern age of bath design. In these pieces we still see different cultural styles: the sensual contours favored in French production; the sturdy mass and tailored geometry of English fittings, and the American penchant for bold, overscale profiles, diminished ornament, and glamorous heft. We can track the historical shift from nickel to easy-maintenance chrome, the eternal luxury and stability of gold, and the salvaged luster of brass showing beneath worn nickel, stripped and buffed and introduced as a finish in its own right.

Fittings also document the evolution of the bath. The merging of dual hot and cold taps into one mixed channel is a French invention much in keeping with that country's appreciation of convenience. Even today the more puritanical English temperament sticks to a division of hot and cold taps. The expediency of the upright shower marks the arrival of twentieth-century velocity in the bath ritual.

The result of all this good industry is a wealth of fitting options. Handles can be spoked or levered, angular or rounded. Plumbing can be neatly concealed or proudly exposed – an early convention now being revived for its forthright display of function. Hand showers bring a similar return of luxury to the bath. Showerheads have grown to the size of sunflowers. Faucet profiles can be high or low, with the sweeping arches of gooseneck spouts or the straightforward sculpture of tubes. Turnings and trimmings have never been more beautifully detailed.

The finest fittings offer refined proportions and consistent shapes or motifs across an entire suite. Mechanically, seals are water-tight, movements never abrupt. The fit in the hand is ergonomic.

The choice of finishes – weathered, brushed, matte, or shiny – further defines the style. Colors run the gamut from gold to rosy copper to all the cool and warm tones of stainless steel, chrome, nickel, and silver. Shade and texture, even more than silhouette, are important to the overall look of the bathroom and should be considered early in design discussions.

No tub system is complete without a hand shower. This flexible component allows optimal range and direction of spray to rinse body and hair as well as the tub basin after use.

ENVIRONMENT

When you envision fittings in the environment of a lavatory, tub, or shower, take care to select forms that clear the edge of the fixture and that leave room for the body. A faucet must extend far enough into a basin so that the water stream drops cleanly into the drain; it must also be high enough off the deck so that the user's hands can fit comfortably beneath it. If the spout needs to cover a wide bowl, it might pivot; if its receiving basin is used for washing hair, it should arch up rather than cantilever out, to create enough space for the head. Gooseneck profiles allow the freest movement because they rise above the bowl and deliver water from an exceptional height; lower pier and semicircular profiles produce a tighter fit and more limited range of motion, necessitating a deeper bowl.

In the bath or shower, heads and sprays may be articulated – that is, constructed with multiple joints. This allows you to direct the jet of water precisely where you want it. Manipulation of the jet is especially pertinent to hand showers, which are useful not only for rinsing the body and hair, but also for cleaning the fixture after you bathe. Hand showers permit the greatest amount of angling into crevices and corners that would be hard to reach with a stationary stream.

In showers the head should be positioned so that you can stand comfortably under the spray of water without stooping. The height of the setting should also allow you to keep your head out of the spray if you don't want to get your hair wet. Moreover, the valve that turns the shower on should be placed at a comfortable height, compatible with the natural reach of your arm. There are no standard elevations here – the shower is always custom-designed, so take advantage of this flexibility to make sure the setting accommodates your own preferences and posture.

FABRICATION

Fittings that are fabricated based upon quality design rather than efficiency of production will yield far cleaner and more beautiful lines and greater ergonomic function than their mass-produced counterparts. These advantages are the result of skillful hand-assembling, where every specialized component and subtle turn of profile is crafted to reach its ideal form. Machine production sacrifices this level of detail and sensitivity to craftsmanship in order to deliver a less costly product; but it will show over the life of the fitting in a clumsier line and less durable operation.

Handcrafted fittings, by comparison, are devoid of crude flares. Their silhouettes are uninterrupted by awkward joints. Proportions are impeccable. These forms are characterized by easy curves and crisp angles. The metal is strong and functional, but it appeals because of its smooth articulation and modeled shape.

Once assembled, high-caliber fittings go through specialized stages of plating and hand-polishing to achieve a dense, ultrasmooth surface. Much like layered wood veneers, finished and polished metal conveys nuances of detail, a crisp edge, and a finely honed texture that can't be achieved by machines.

When choosing fittings, look for signs of artisanal craftsmanship: a sculptural shape with seamless lines and a satisfying integrity and weight in hand. Examine items closely to identify the continuous brilliant luster and supple surface that are trademarks of hand-polishing. Fittings from England, France, and Germany are often of the highest quality, since artisanal methods of fabrication have been maintained there over generations in many small factories.

care

The lustrous finish on beautifully crafted fittings should be treated with the same care one would devote to the finish of a well-loved car. Improper handling or cleaning can damage the surface of the fitting, and careless upkeep is a sure way to allow air and water to ravage a protective metal coating.

In most plumbing systems, traces of acid and other minerals will be left on the surface of a fitting after the water has evaporated. Lime will collect into white deposits, iron can cause brown stains, and acid will etch the metal. Acid levels can also break down copper residues in the pipes, leading to green stains. Sunlight will dull and yellow a finish over time, and air will oxidize and tarnish metal.

The best way to prevent deposits from forming is to wipe the fitting dry immediately after use. Simply rub it gently with a soft damp cloth and wipe it dry with a soft towel. If necessary, use only a mild soap solution in combination with warm water. The use of abrasive cleaners, solvents, ammonia, vinegar, or other acidic agents will degrade the finish and, in virtually all cases, void any warranty on the fitting.

Pure carnauba car wax with no additive cleaning agents will also help protect the finish from mineral deposits. When the water stops beading on the finish, it is time for a fresh wax application.

Beyond these general instructions, certain metals require different types and frequency of maintenance. Of all the finish metals, chrome is the most durable and easiest to preserve, followed by nickel. These metals require little conservation other than basic wiping and waxing. Silver-plated finishes will tarnish with age, an effect that you may or may not desire. You can restore silver to its original luster by using a nonabrasive silver polish. In the same way, unlacquered brass and copper finishes will change over time, though these metals oxidize far more quickly. Appropriate polishing compounds will restore their luster, but be aware that upkeep will be time-consuming and perpetual. By contrast, lumin, a relatively new finish, captures the look of clean brass or gold and doesn't tarnish. This metal should be maintained only with a soft cloth; brass polish will fatally strip the finish.

Left untouched, brass, copper, and bronze will develop a mottled, multicolored patina that can be very beautiful. If you plan for this type of finish in your installation, you can also choose from a variety of weathered metals that will continue to season and mellow with age.

surfacing

SURFACING IS ANY MEDIUM USED TO CREATE OR COVER A WALL, FLOOR, OR COUNTERTOP. AS A VEHICLE FOR COLOR, PATTERN, AND DECORATION, IT HAS THE GREATEST OVERLAP OF USE FROM ONE KIND OF INTERIOR SPACE TO ANOTHER. BUT IN THE BATH INSTALLATION IT REMAINS UNIQUELY ENVIRONMENTAL, RESTRICTED NOT ONLY BY A NEED TO RESIST WATER BUT ALSO BY THE CONCERNS OF DURABILITY, TRACTION, AND HYGIENE. CAN A SURFACE WITHSTAND WATER PRESSURE WITHOUT CRACKING OR BUCKLING? IS IT GRADED WELL ENOUGH TO GRAB AND HOLD A BARE FOOT? IS IT EASY TO WIPE CLEAN? WILL IT DRY QUICKLY? IS IT OPAQUE, PROVIDING MODESTY, OR IS IT TRANSLUCENT, ADMITTING LIGHT?

These considerations make the choice of materials crucial. Over centuries, bathroom surfaces have been well chosen to meet the demands of this damp environment. Today they range from classic ceramic tile, stone, terra-cotta, and certain woods to poured cement, molded resin, and cast glass.

Surfacing is also important to the overall style and is often the starting point for the visual tone and attitude of the space. Motif, ornament, texture, and palette prevail here over the constant givens of the room's equipment – the fixtures and fittings.

Of the bathroom essentials, surface covering is the only element that is independent of human scale. It can be constructed of pieces no bigger than a thumbnail, or it may be laid in one continuous expanse. It is the practice of repetition and breadth, fragment and amplitude, that gives the architecture its selective melody.

Because surfacing is a construction, it is critical to work with an experienced contractor and a knowledgeable team of craftspeople who understand your site and can guide you through a sound installation.

Every surface should be laid out first on paper, so that there is a working blueprint to follow when materials are fixed in place. A tile pattern will definitely require detailed measurements of your space and should be tested with a dry layout to plot cuts, fields, and corner treatments. The placement of fixtures and fittings will directly affect the distribution of pattern in any surface – including slabs and cladding – so it is crucial to review the full specs of your site with your installer to underscore where and how those masses will factor into each physical plane.

Following these design concerns, a brief primer on methods of installation is useful to help you communicate successfully with your team. Foremost among these is a *mud set, or wet bed, installation*. This technique is a necessity in sites with uneven walls and floors – in particular, old houses – but it can be used in any location to give the installer supreme control over both the environment and the surfacing element. With this technique, any waves and dips in the construction are first leveled out with a cement mixture; then, an appropriate amount of cement is laid over the substrate, floor, or wall to create a bed for the material. Mud set is the preferred method when the tile to be installed is ungauged, like slate or antique terra-cotta, or when it has an uneven thickness.

A *thin set installation* is appropriate for sites with plumb, level planes, but it can be employed only within certain material and substrate tolerances. This method produces a setting bed that is usually $\frac{1}{8}$ to $\frac{1}{4}$ inch thick, using a mixture of cement, sand, and other agents to which water is added. This adhesive is troweled over the subfloor or wall and/or buttered on the back of each surfacing slab or tile, creating a uniform bond.

A *medium, or mortar bed, installation* is heavier and more viscous than thin set, allowing a thicker floor to be built up. The mortar bed will support heavy stones without slumping during the curing process.

Mastic installations use a glue to adhere materials to walls and floors. This setting technique is best used for ceramic tile walls; it should never be used with stone floor installations. Oil-based mastics should not be used with stone in any application, as they are likely to stain the material.

With any of these methods, your installer should also advise you on an appropriate adhesive so that the setting bed does not discolor the material that goes on top of it.

Investing in skilled craftsmen for these tasks will ensure the meticulous presentation of each surface. Find competent workers through your architect or designer and show respect for their advice, for beautiful materials alone are only the visible half of a successful installation; the rest depends on talented labor.

showers

THE SHOWER IS THE NEWEST AND OFTEN THE MOST IMAGINATIVE SETTING TO EMERGE IN THE BATHROOM LANDSCAPE. IT IS A ROOM WITHIN THE ROOM; NOT SO MUCH A FIXTURE, ALTHOUGH IT MUST CONTAIN THE BODY, AS A UNIQUE COALITION OF SURFACING AND FITTINGS. THIS IS AN AREA WHERE CUSTOM PLUMBING OPTIONS ARE NUMEROUS, WHERE IDIOSYNCRASIES IN THE FLOOR PLAN CAN BE TURNED INTO DESIGN ADVANTAGES, AND WHERE AN INVENTIVE USE OF MATERIALS CAN CATAPULT AN ORDINARY SPACE INTO THE REALM OF THE EXCEPTIONAL.

The shower is often perceived as a more utilitarian zone than the tub, and so hosts a different kind of practical routine. But as people increasingly devote energy to this station as the primary bathing environment, the shower has earned a new autonomous status and a right to prime square footage in many installations. Stalls have grown more spacious and opulent, sometimes even displacing the once-inevitable tub in small bathrooms that can't accommodate two facilities.

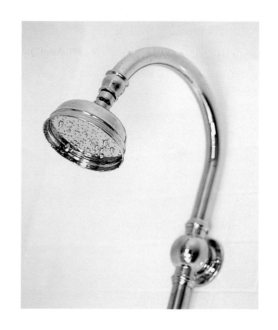

Shower fittings, too, are now available in an unprecedented range of designs and degrees of luxury. Today one can choose from showerheads and hoses of every diameter and shape, with a number of adjustable settings. Thermostatic valves can be set automatically to a preferred temperature every time the water is turned on; a water-friendly teak seat can be installed for the comfort of a longer shower and to provide a platform for shaving legs. Diverters off the main pipeline can accommodate the extra stream of a handheld shower. Brought together, these elements constitute a superb shower experience.

Other devices can turn the shower into a virtual home spa. Vertical spray bars and individual body sprays will deliver a toning hydromassage. Steam heat can be piped into enclosed stalls, promoting perspiration to cleanse pores, and drawing therapeutic moisture into both the lungs and skin. Large showerheads can be mounted on the ceiling for a flood of water that will envelop the whole body.

Whichever features you prefer, it is important to commit to them at the outset of a shower installation; later additions will be nearly impossible without stripping the surfacing off the walls. A built-in shower seat, for example, will call for proper backing in the wall, and steam heat will require a separate pipeline into the stall as well as a properly sealed shower door.

If your shower is to have its own storage, there are additional architectural fixtures to consider. You'll need racks and shelves for shampoos, soaps, and other accoutrements – no more stooping in the corner for the slippery bottle; the space should allow you to stand up straight, with products at an arm's reach.

As important as these details are, they do not restrict the design of the surrounding space. The shower can be as stimulating or as calm as its materials – a pastorale of mosaic vines or a sleek fuselage of glass, marble, or cement. It can be encased or left open to the rest of the room, sunk below floor level or raised on a platform, camouflaged behind screens opaque or clear, flexible or rigid. It can be an armature of curves, a boxy cabin, or a hexagonal or rectangular podium. It can return outdoors as an open-air chamber for rinsing off summer sand and ocean salt.

No matter what the format, the shower is always a live event. It is a place enveloped in the sound of a downpour, with water sluicing over the skin in a continuous massaging torrent. Far more than the suspended animation of a good bath, showering revives and energizes the senses.

If space and routine require that you combine tub and shower, consider using an architectural enclosure like glass doors in place of a loose curtain above the tub rim. The rigid plane here implies a wall, effectively creating a room within the room.

In the broadest sense, organizing the bath for storage is no different from organizing a kitchen or office. All are highly functional spaces with major equipment, yet they require many additional elements to function properly. A parallel can be drawn between spices, foodstuffs, and dishes; papers, pens, and computer disks; towels, soaps, and shampoos. Combining these items into a logical structure determines how well, and ultimately how attractively, the room will work on a daily basis.

A wealth of bath design opportunities exist in the intervals between major fixtures. Shelves, cupboards, and bins tucked into these spaces will do much to determine how this room is laid out for daily function: where to keep towels, tissues, toilet paper, razors, toothbrushes, and soaps. Are these secondary fixtures built in or movable, open or closed, consistent with the room's basic materials, like metal and porcelain accessories, or distinct from them, like baskets, hampers, and furniture? Faced with the scores of loose items you'll need in the bath routine, how can you strike the right balance between utility and decoration?

How these questions are answered can enhance or thwart your use of the room. And crucial to this performance is the design of storage, where ideally all of your towels, cosmetics, and the like are stored in the most practical place. This means that items you use with the help of a mirror should be stored near the mirror, that hand towels and washcloths should be placed close to the lavatory bowl, that bath towels and mats should be kept within easy reach of the tub or shower. Planning good storage also means thinking ahead: provide a wastebasket and a laundry hamper, a tray or dish for jewelry, and a well-ventilated area where wet towels can be hung after use, so that they dry out fully.

You'll also want to assess how various items will stand up in the watery environment of the bath. Paper packaging for medicines, sundries, and soaps can stain and shred when wet; metal canisters, hairpins, tweezers, scissors, and combs can rust. Items like these should be stored behind glass or in cabinets and drawers, so you'll need to introduce those forms of storage as part of your structural blueprint.

In laying out the bath for storage, it is important to be aware of the assets and limitations of different types of fixtures. The style of your lavatory, tub, and shower will determine how much counter space and shelving the room can hold and as a result will largely prescribe how much additional storage needs to be added to the overall design.

Each major decision will affect every other, so look at how they work together. If a fixture reduces storage space – a pedestal lavatory in lieu of a console, for example, or a freestanding tub rather than a deck installation – where will you put the displaced supplies? What will happen with shelving if prime wall space is fronted by a major fixture? If several people will be using the room, how extensive is each person's bath inventory? Will competing products clutter the available counter space? Do they need to be put away or displayed in some visual order?

Since these concerns tend to be hidden during the drafting stages of a design, it is useful to walk through the raw space of your installation and get a feel for how a projected layout will fill the room. This exercise should take place while you are shopping for the principal architectural elements, so that you can adjust the floor plan based on each choice you make.

Your current bath is also a valuable source of information, as it is a concrete example of what works and doesn't work. Look for the successful details that you want to repeat, and for the failures or shortcomings you want to avoid. Keep your decisions grounded in this reality, for no matter how appealing each fixture looks in a showroom, and how sensible a blueprint provided by your architect or designer, only you know how much storage you will need in practice.

{exploring} storage

Once you determine the best places for storage, the particular forms that you choose will depend on personal taste. From jars and bins to furniture and fixtures, the clearest differences in style have to do with visibility and concealment.

With concealed storage, the contents of a unit are hidden or camouflaged. Drawers, cabinets, closets, hampers, and containers made of wood, leather, wicker, and metal make good hiding places. Concealed storage produces a neat, uncluttered environment.

If your concealed storage is primarily built in, as in, for example, an enclosed lavatory console, a wall-mounted and recessed medicine cabinet, or closets, the bath will assume a spare, gallerylike appearance. Such a room can be adapted to sleek modern materials like brushed steel or chrome; opaque, ribbed, or colored glass; and polished wood or wood veneers. You could also create a rustic effect with the use of honed woods, distressed paint finishes, and weathered metals.

A newer approach for concealed storage is to import freestanding furniture into the bath. This creates a more dynamic interior and liberates a design from typical storage elements like mirrored medicine cabinets and shelving. Ideal for this look are stainless-steel medical and dental cases, which are durable and impervious to water and grime (older pieces with remnant enamel or paint should be sealed to prevent rust). Fine woodworked forms like credenzas, cases, and hutches make a direct reference to the other rooms of a house.

Following this track, new designs are emerging that scale down traditional furniture pieces to meet the smaller dimensions of most bathrooms. These elements, including wash tables with cabinets, lockers, cases, and chests, combine a strong decorative look with practicality and versatility. The finishes are water-resistant, and the bantam sizes allow rooms with no built-ins to incorporate basic closed storage.

In any design, concealed storage allows each object that *is* displayed to be viewed as an artifact rather than a routine accessory. A potted orchid, a collection of perfume bottles, a cluster of candles, a crisp row of towels on a hanging bar — even a few of these elements will prevent the space from appearing stark or clinical. On the other end of the design spectrum, exposed storage uses conspicuous display to reveal the room's accessories. This approach requires an ongoing commitment to organization and a talent for composition and placement, but at its best it can invest a space with warmth and character.

Open shelving is the most common type of exposed storage. This format can keep counters free of clutter and compensate for pedestal lavatories or a freestanding tub with no peripheral deck.

Built-in or recessed shelves can make the most of an unused expanse of wall without compromising valuable floor space, and can be deep and tall enough to hold stacks of towels, textiles, interesting containers, rows of toilet paper, glassware, and even art objects. This type of storage delivers a perfect fusion of style and function and gives an installation an expansive, loftlike feel.

Wall-mounted or cantilevered shelves tend to be no more than 8 or 9 inches deep, so they are best used for smaller supplies and decorative objects. Like recessed shelves, however, they can run any length, provided they have appropriate braces or backing in the wall. Wall-mounted shelves work well in high-traffic areas that require basic storage — over the lavatory or water closet. In the absence of a medicine cabinet, some flat mirrors come framed with an outcrop ledge, effectively creating a shelf at a useful height above the counter.

FLAT MIRROR VERSUS MEDICINE CABINET

The bathroom mirror, for most of the twentieth century, was attached to a medicine cabinet. Now, however, it is increasingly being replaced by the autonomous flat mirror – a shift that puts design in competition with traditional storage needs.

Flat mirrors are appearing with greater frequency today because they can be framed, shaped, and lit more decoratively and because they can be bigger. These larger mirrors not only offer an expanded field of view but also help to balance out the span of an overscale vanity or console. In this way the wall treatment remains most proportionate to the mass of the given fixture.

Style selections for this approach are numerous. The mirror can be square, circular, or polygonal; it can be mechanical or fixed, buttressed out from the wall or set flush into it. The frame can match or complement other design materials or highlight a singular, dramatic motif. Thus a simple chrome or wood molding could echo the lines and materials of a washstand, an austere space could be enlivened by a massive gilt-framed mirror, or a floral-etched Venetian mirror could stand sentinel over a brushed-steel console. As with a painting, the frame finishes the environment and gives it visual emphasis.

On the downside, flat mirrors lack the concealed storage space contained in a mirrored medicine cabinet, so the unattractive items that routinely collect there will have to be relocated. Small freestanding drawer units, vanity cabinets, and medical cases will keep provisions close to the lavatory basin without exposing the landscape to clutter.

Medicine cabinets put storage first, but they are available in fewer designs. These forms suggest a very familiar bath decoration and are a must in installations where there is no space for an auxiliary piece of furniture.

A traditional medicine cabinet can echo the unobtrusive look of a flat mirror if it is recessed into the wall. It will disappear as a fixture altogether if door pulls are replaced by sliding plates. Or it can be installed as a wall-mounted hutch, bringing some dimension and variation to the vertical plane. This can be a useful design element in a very simple installation with modest fixtures.

Wall-mounted cabinets are usually made of either wood or metal. The finish might be a weathered or distressed wood stain, suggesting a rustic motif, or plain white paint, which works well in a tone-on-tone room with lots of ceramic tile. Some wood cabinets may also extend their storage benefits with the addition of a hanging towel bar – an especially useful feature in conjunction with a pedestal or console lavatory that has no integral towel rails.

By comparison, a polished chrome medicine cabinet suggests a sleek midcentury design and helps to preserve the mirror, rather than its frame, as the object of focus. Vintage metal cabinets often come in attractive shapes and may have interesting etching around the perimeter of the mirror, adding some personality and ornamentation to an otherwise plain construction.

PEDESTAL VERSUS ENCLOSED LAVATORY

Storage capacity is also a significant consideration in choosing a lavatory. Along with its neighboring medicine cabinet, this is the station where the broadest number of supplies will accumulate and where countertops and shelves are the most open to variation.

Silhouette also comes into play with washstands. In these designs, storage space can be augmented by incorporating trestle shelves and towel railings into the frame. In slab-top washstands, of course, counter space can be expanded to any custom length.

Because washstands are open and linear, they possess less mass and thus appear lighter than porcelain consoles, even though their storage volume is greater. The combination of additional storage and diminished bulk makes these forms suitable for installation in small spaces.

In bathrooms large and small, cabinetry installed around a lavatory produces optimal concealed storage. With a modest-size basin, the deck space may not increase greatly, but the shelving beneath will create a home for provisions and will also serve to mask exposed pipes. The cabinet can be as large as space allows, permitting the installation of handsome built-in vanities with drawers, bins, shelves, and generous stretches of countertop.

The success of all of these selections will depend on the area where the lavatory will be situated. The density and enclosure of cabinetry may serve to balance the distribution of mass in the rest of the room, or fill a nook nicely so that it appears flush with a wall. In a narrow space, a less weighted base or pedestal with an exposed line might be more suitable, with storage placed elsewhere. The room's architecture will affect the way a lavatory suits its site, compressing around it for a fitted feel or allowing it to float as a solitary fixture.

Pedestal lavatories have the least available supply space; enclosed vanities have the most. The pedestal style offers a refined sculptural silhouette that fits neatly into a small area and hides under-mounted pipes for a very finished look, but it provides little counter space around the basin and no cabinet space beneath. If you choose this design, it is crucial to integrate other storage elements into the area. Good choices include towel bars, exposed shelving, recessed medicine cabinets, and freestanding furniture. Shelves directly above the pedestal provide the most practical home for those supplies and accessories that would normally be placed on the counter near the basin.

Retaining the classical look of a pedestal lavatory, porcelain consoles increase the visual mass of the fixture and tend to have expanded deck space for key provisions. These features are pluses in larger rooms, where basic storage can be distributed into other exposed or concealed units, permitting the silhouette of the lavatory to remain pure and undisrupted in its contours from basin to leg.

ACCESSORIES

The racks, bars, hooks, and rings that hold towels all function as exposed storage. This type of storage also includes ceramic soap dishes and toothbrush holders affixed above the lavatory, as well as wire soap baskets and caddies in the shower or tub. The placement of these pieces requires thoughtful design consideration, since they should ensure a permanent, dedicated stock of supplies. They can also keep counters free of clutter. This produces a clean look that recalls the baths of the mid–twentieth century, when built-in elements emphasized a space-saving efficiency of design.

Drawing upon English and French custom, the use of metal wiring to hold soaps and other items combines high-style design with ease of maintenance. Unlike ceramic trays and recesses, which catch and hold soap residues and must be cleaned frequently, wire forms allow excess lather to drain automatically and can be kept in pristine condition with a few jets of water from a hand shower. Such elements, of course, must be installed over a tub, shower, or lavatory, or provided with an under-shell of glass or porcelain, so that water does not pool or drip onto counters.

In order to achieve a more flexible design, many of the same functions can be served by freestanding pieces. These elements include formal bath accessories as well as tumblers, trays, cups, and dishes. A beautiful etched fountain glass can become a holder for toothbrushes and toothpaste; a hand-carved horn dish or a scallop shell could serve as a decorative holder for soap. A tiered stand or ladder for towels can be placed between a tub and shower stall in a space that might not accommodate a larger piece of furniture.

Choices like these emphasize an interior rather than a bath-oriented style and open up even the tiniest spaces to a wider range of textures, forms, and materials. Because they reveal individual character and taste, not only in their design but also in their placement, these elements showcase rather than minimize the items they're designed to hold.

TRANSPARENCY

In cabinetry, whether built in or freestanding, glass-paned doors often appear in combination with concealed cabinets below. The glass relieves the solid expanses of paneling or metal for a more varied material palette and allows decorative objects to be displayed to break up the flat plane of the unit. Glass-fronted bookcases and vitrines are especially good choices for storing towels and other attractive items.

Beyond furniture, glass containers, from handblown urns to hardy Pyrex jars, are ideal for holding swabs, cotton balls, colored soaps, sponges — ordinary goods presented as functional sculpture.

Other utilitarian items like makeup brushes, combs and hairbrushes, and toothbrushes can also provide enlivening detail for a bathroom when stored openly. Because these items should be left in the open air, the containers they're put in can be fashioned of almost any material — from clear to translucent to opaque, from glass to alabaster, from wood to leather — as long as they are not enclosed.

Whether behind glass or on open shelves, exposed storage is always an exercise in texture. Towels can be organized to create a sort of textural composition — an oblong stack here, a square-sided pile there. The same towels can be rolled up and fashioned into a pyramid or a layered stack: hand towel on bath towel, washcloth on top, a bar of soap as terminus. Toilet paper rolls can be stacked neatly in rows or tossed randomly into a big basket. The bathroom naturally incorporates products that possess appealing sculptural form and that can usefully be stored in multiples. Making displays of these basic commodities can soften the slick shell of the room and at the same time simplify its use: if something is on view, it's easy to find.

CONTAINING CLUTTER

The easiest way to manage clutter in the bath is to choose concealed storage. But even when using exposed storage, a few basic techniques will help you maintain order.

If shelving is your main storage system, you can use multiple units of crates, bins, or trays to house different products — medicines and pharmaceuticals in one, lotions and sunscreens in another, hair dryers and curlers in the next, and so on. Organizing these loose items into similar containers simplifies any bathroom's design because the repetition produces a soothing symmetry. For a more dynamic display, you can introduce a disparate element into the sequence — a stack of towels, perhaps, a few oversized bottles, or a group of candles.

Another tactic involves removing items from their packaging and storing them in attractive containers. This eliminates the visual competition between often mundane product graphics and replaces it with a far cleaner presentation: the items may either be exposed in glass containers, or stored in interesting canisters and jars. This approach is especially useful for small items like hairpins, razor blades, and cosmetics.

These strategies result in a mix of concealed and exposed storage, which represents the best solution for placement of goods in the bath: it creates enough texture for the space to have interest, and enough order for it to be serene.

elements

A BATH INSTALLATION IS ONLY AS GOOD

AS THE MATERIALS THAT GO INTO IT. IN THIS ENVIRONMENT, QUALITY IS PAR-

TICULARLY IMPORTANT BECAUSE EACH MATERIAL MUST PERFORM DIRECTLY

UNDER THE ERODING FORCE OF WATER. QUALITY, CUT, AND HONESTY OF

CRAFTSMANSHIP ARE NOT SIMPLY A MATTER OF STYLE; THEY ARE YOUR ASSUR-

ANCE THAT EACH MEDIUM IS AT ITS SOUNDEST AND MOST DURABLE AND IS

ASSIGNED TO THE AREA WHERE IT WILL DO THE BEST JOB.

In this room we are treated to the look of pure elements – the glint of metal, the solidity of stone, the liquidity of glass. Here we see clay hardened by fire, cotton spun into terry cloth, the essence of plants and flowers suspended in salt, aromatic in beeswax and soap. Every article exists in a one-to-one correlation with the elemental body, with water. A sensitivity to these basic materials is crucial in creating a tasteful, well-balanced bathroom. If you take time to explore their individual properties, it will become much easier to manage their combined effects in the ensuing design process.

The textures that animate the bathroom derive directly from the quality of the materials used in installation. As a rule, natural materials have a richer texture than synthetics. That difference is what makes stone or wood so much more vital than Formica, glass more bewitching than plastic, sea sponges and sable hairbrushes more luxurious than polymers. Natural materials will feel warmer and more substantial and will generally improve in character over time; unlike synthetics, they can develop patina over long years of use.

In terms of budget, natural materials will surprise you. A space clad in wood, stone, ceramic, or glass will cost no more, and sometimes less, than one done in high-performance synthetics. Moreover, these materials have a greater range of finishes, making them adaptable to innumerable textures. It is a common misperception to equate "natural" with "rustic"; but these same materials can be crafted to appear streamlined, lustrous, and refined.

Two major exceptions to this standard are the use of acrylics for bathtubs and of translucent resins for accessories and futuristic countertops. The look and lightness of resins have no direct natural counterpart, but this material has the practical benefit of being shatterproof. It is also receptive to color, especially tints and washes in a pale beach-glass range.

Beyond material, there is finish. The mark of the hand in an artisanal finish can produce a texture unmatchable by machines. The most durable surface materials are thus often the most authentic, especially if the fabrication communicates a human attention to detail, harmony, and composition.

metal

METAL IS A MATERIAL OF SUPREME STRENGTH, YET IT APPEARS AS FLUID AS WATER. IT IS A MEDIUM OF TOOLED PRECISION, BOTH LIQUID AND SOLID: THE INTEGRAL GEAR OF THE BATHROOM.

Metal is sculpturally efficient. It can be cast, forged, bent, hammered, or perforated; it can be polished or coated with another metal. Always streamlined, this element may be finished in a range of colors and lusters that will invigorate the mechanics of plumbing.

All metal will be burnished over time by continual rubbing and wear. This patina can give metal an attractive warmth and texture. By contrast, antique metal pieces, like the vintage medicine cabinets and vanities that are in demand today, can be refinished to a sleek silvery steel or brilliant chrome that makes a very modern design statement.

Metal has as great a range of tone and radiance as any color family. Brass can be a lush verdigris or a vivid gold; bronze carries sepia overtones. Nickel offers a satiny warmth compared to the hard icy blue of chrome. Silver reflects white. Copper is the color of flame.

Metal's variance of luster – its coolness or warmth, reflection or saturation – adds to its beauty and makes it one of the most dynamic elements in any installation. For example, an old worn nickel faucet is across the spectrum from a highly polished tub mixer clad in the same material. With its changing tonality, metal can thread different colors together and introduce a layer of light into the decoration that will animate the room's mass and textures.

ceramic

O F ALL THE ELEMENTS IN THE BATHROOM, CERAMICS HAVE THE MOST WIDE-SPREAD APPLICATION. THIS MOST MALLEABLE OF RAW MATERIALS CAN BE FASHIONED INTO COUNTLESS SHAPES, INCLUDING THE SMOOTH SURFACES, TEXTURED PLANES, CURVILINEAR BASINS, AND GEOMETRIC TILES THAT CLAD THE ROOM WALLS AND MOST OF ITS FIXTURES.

This material is so popular because it is so inherently clean. In a room designed for health and hygiene, high-fired glazed clay is a nonporous material that inhibits the absorption of bacteria and dirt. More durable than glass, ceramic surfaces shed water and are inclined to wick away dirt. As a result, they are extremely easy to clean. Any number of detergents and disinfectants can be used on ceramics without compromising their stability, elegance, or durability.

In vitreous china and in tile, a ceramic surface will reflect light, lending to the bath a freshness and sparkle that make the room feel sanitary.

Under this immaculate seal, the material works its wonders with color: no other medium appears so thoroughly white, so saturated or painterly and ethereal of hue. Ceramics absorb color and bounce it, giving the bath the energy and tone of a painted canvas.

terra-cotta

TERRA-COTTA LITERALLY MEANS "COOKED EARTH."

No surfacing material is more basic or more beautiful than this raw clay baked to a hardy earthen finish.

Though it is neither stone nor ceramic, terra-cotta possesses many of each material's best qualities: stone's elemental purity and natural coloration, ceramic's variation in texture and shape. And since terra-cotta is fired for a long time to strengthen its bisque state, it possesses an innate durability and an organic texture that make it very supportive underfoot. Traditionally sealed with linseed oil and up to six coats of wax, the surface acquires a leathery patina that continues to deepen with age. Vintage terra-cotta tiles, salvaged from courtyards and homes throughout France, Italy, Spain, and Latin America, have a nearly fossilized luster that is breathtaking, capturing the weathering of decades in the sun and rain.

The regional clays used to produce terra-cotta tiles yield a surprising and complex range of shades, from smoky bronze to intense rusty brick to luminous yellow. Different types of fuel used to fire terra-cotta also affect the finish and texture of the final tile: in the South of France, for example, tiles are fired in wood-burning kilns; in Mexico, they are dried and cured in the sun. Other producers use gas-fired kilns, which produce a more regular finish that emphasizes the inherent tonality of the clay.

Used as the basis of a natural palette for the bathroom, terra-cotta gives walls and floors a rustic softness and depth. The material instantly appears ancient and warm, evoking an outdoor atmosphere and a sense of sunny leisure.

stone

S TONE IS AS RICHLY FIXED BY NATURE AS CERAMICS ARE UNBOUND

BY IT. USED IN MANY OF THE SAME APPLICATIONS, STONE IS ALL HARD

PLANES AND STRAIGHT EDGES. WHETHER POLISHED TO A HIGH SHEEN

OR LEFT TUMBLED AND RUGGED, THIS MATERIAL WILL ALWAYS APPEAR

ELEMENTAL, DEFINITIVE, AND RESTRAINED. STONE IS UNMISTAKABLY

STONE, FATED TO RETAIN THE RAW IMPRINT OF THE ROCK FROM WHICH

IT WAS CUT.

From soft, honed limestone and slate in deep earth tones to silken white marble, stone has long been valued for its visual opulence. The finite quantities and labor-intensive process of quarrying, cutting, sculpting, and polishing stone add to this material's inherent luxury. As a result, stone's presence in the bath – whether as slab, mosaic, vessel, or cladding – can signify a classicism that no other material can match.

Because the surface of stone is imperfect and porous, each spill and footprint will subtly change it. The glass set down without a coaster, the oily drops of candle wax, the stains and wear of water – every incident is part of a personal history that gets embedded in the material. Stone has none of the stability of glass, ceramic tile, or paint, nor will it produce a regular, solid field; it is inherently patterned, striated with intricate veins and mineral washes that ebb and surge over every square inch of its surface. Stone's beauty lies in this variation and evolution. If you appreciate its environmental quality and modality, its organic range of color and matrix, living with it as it ages can be a wonderful experience.

The tonal and textural character of any stone is an outcome of how the material is formed in the ground. Modes of synthesis vary according to the type of stone family.

Limestone and *marble* — the two most common families of stone used for surfacing — begin as the same substance. Both stones are composed of sedimentary material (largely seashells and bones of sea creatures), which collected over a period of 300 million years on the ocean floor. This composition is the reason that fossils are visible in certain types of limestone. The calcium in those bones combined with the carbon dioxide in the water produces calcium carbonite, the basic mineral structure of all limestone and marble.

Limestone results from the pressure of layers of earth covering this sediment table, an evolution spanning another 50 million years. Where there was additional heat and pressure — melting and recooling the sediment — the limestone crystallized, becoming marble. By technical definition, marble is simply transformed limestone.

It is necessary for a stone to have been crystallized in order for it to have a polished or reflective surface. For this reason, marble can polish but limestone cannot. Limestone has a large grain structure that cannot be ground perfectly flat — the state in which a material reflects light purely — whereas, because of its altered crystalline structure, marble has a smooth consistency that permits flat grinding. This is not the only way to finish marble, however: the material can also be honed by using coarser abrasives in the polishing process. These finishing methods are akin to sanding wood with different gauges of paper — the grain itself remains smooth and integral, while the surface texture yields to varying degrees of fineness or roughness.

Travertine is another class of stone that shares traits of both limestone and marble. This material is formed in areas where percolating water has bubbled up through the sediment, leaving the rock with small pocks and holes that are consistent with the granular matrix of limestone. (These holes can be left open or filled in with cementious material to produce a level surface.)

At the same time, travertines are crystallized stones and so can be polished. This composition creates an interesting duality of surface and grain, where a dense, textured stone can be finished with the smoothness and reflection of marble.

All stone is harvested in a quarrying process — cutting into an exposed face of rock that has been cleared of overlaying soil. Like wine, each stone bears the unique impression of the terrain from which it derives, and qualities are so named for the specific regions or countries where they are quarried. Famous and prized examples, such as the lustrous white marble from Carrara, Italy, have been sourced continually from the same villages for thousands of years; other veins have been exhausted, their stone now extinct save for vintage slabs and tiles.

A raw stone block, as cut from a quarry, will typically measure 6 feet wide to 6 to 7 feet high to 8 feet long. These blocks are then taken to fabricating plants for cutting into formal tiles and slabs. Tiles are commonly produced from smaller 12-by-8-inch strips, while slabs can vary in size and thickness according to the block from which they are cut. Fabrication plants can produce custom pieces of almost any size and dimension.

On the diminutive end of the stone spectrum are mosaics and terrazzo, the latter the result of a traditional Italian technique in which chips of marble are set in cement and polished to a smooth plane.

Because it can be laid in a seamless expanse or molded to any size and shape, terrazzo can achieve a look as modern as its method is ancient. New resin polymers as well as glass and other types of aggregate stone echo the appearance of marble with further contemporary options of color and texture.

COLORATION

All stones are cut with water running over the raw block. This is especially pertinent to stone tiles, which are packed immediately after cutting while they are still thoroughly wet. Stone tiles will stay wet in their sealed boxes or crates until they are unpacked for installation, at which time they may appear much darker than the shade lot of a showroom sample. As a general rule, wet tiles look five times darker than dry ones; the tiles will dry and stabilize over two weeks. This fluctuation also applies to installation itself, as stone tiles will draw moisture from the setting bed and may turn darker temporarily.

To clear these optical hurdles, let a number of test stones dry fully before installation begins. This is the time to make sure that the delivered lot sits within the shade range you have specified. Once the tiles have stabilized, be prepared for the coloration to vary from piece to piece at least as much as handmade ceramic examples. As with any tile, color gauging and dry layouts will help achieve good control of the palette, with smooth gradations of tone and a balanced, directional sweep of pattern from stone to stone.

FACING

Architectural stone can be finished today in facings that range from slick and clean-edged to rustic and weathered. Such effects are achieved by manipulating the material's surface with different types of machinery and sawing methods. When surveying stone options, it is necessary to check with the vendor to see what types of finishes are available for any sample, taking into account that certain treatments are applicable to only some types of stone and finish technology varies from plant to plant around the world.

Stone finishes are most generally characterized on a spectrum of honed to polished. *Honed finishes* are smooth and matte and are most commonly used with nonreflective limestone to achieve a finely ground surface. *Polished finishes* deliver a reflective, glossy surface and are applicable only to stones (typically marbles and travertines and granites) that have been crystallized.

Flamed finishes apply to very hard limestones and most granites. In this process the face of the stone is heated to a very high temperature, causing the crystals on the surface to explode. The result is a very rough but shallow texture appropriate for high traffic use, including outdoor applications and shower floors.

Tumbled finishes are applicable to virtually all types of stone tile. The tiles, along with pebbles and water, are put into a machine resembling a cement mixer. As the mixer agitates, the materials tumble and bang into one another, leaving the edges and face of each tile with a beaten appearance that recalls ancient or weathered stone.

In a *cobblestone finish*, the face of the tile is smoothly honed, while the edges are distressed or hammered. This technique captures the rounded look of old street pavers. *Pillowed finishes* offer a variation on this effect. The face of the tile is sanded down approximately 1 to 1½ inches from each edge, giving the sides a more pronounced curving slope.

Antiqued finishes accelerate the effects of patina for some stones. In this technique, the face of the tile is acid-washed or hard wire–brushed to sweep away the softer materials in the veins of the stone. Then the tile is ground with an undulating honing machine to give the surface a gently rolling appearance, as if it had been walked on for hundreds of years.

Other methods produce more dimensionally textured surfaces. A *bushammered finish* delivers shallow pockmarks all over the face of the stone, as if a pointed chisel were hammered into the material every quarter inch. In a *sandblasted finish*, air-forced sand is blown onto the face of the stone, pitting the surface in a fine grain. *Sawn finishes*, typically used only with travertine tiles, create a very rough-hewn texture by highlighting the cut marks of the saw blade as it passes through the stone. After this cutting no further finishing is done to the face of the tile save a round of light sanding to eliminate some of the circular marks from the saw.

SEALING

Every type of stone, facing, and application, from tile to slab to cladding, is vulnerable to staining and must be sealed after it's installed. Good sealers will penetrate the surface and fill the pores of the stone, providing a crucial barrier against many foreign substances that can cause blotching and discoloration. Look for products in a clear, matte liquid form that will not alter the finish or luster of the stone.

Sealers are best applied in two coats – one prior to grouting and one after on a thoroughly cleaned floor. Each coat should be allowed to dry for a full twenty-four hours before the surface is exposed to the next phase of installation. As with other types of wood and metal finish care, the sealing process should be repeated periodically over the life of the site, when water stops beading on the face of the stone. Coatings may last up to a year or more depending on the site and frequency of use.

mosaic

MOSAIC IS ONE OF THE MOST DRAMATIC APPLICATIONS OF ARCHITECTURAL STONE. THIS SURFACE'S HAND-LAID TEXTURE AND INTRICATE IRREGULARITY PRODUCE A DECORATION WITH AS MUCH MOVEMENT AS PAINTING BUT WITH A CONSIDERABLY LONGER LIFE SPAN. THE MATERIAL ITSELF CONFERS A PRECIOUS QUALITY TO THE PRACTICE, FOR STONE CUT SO SMALL IS AN ART ALL ITS OWN.

Blending numerous earthen tones with the saturated or rich color of marbles and minerals like lapis and quartz produces a versatile natural palette for mosaic with unsurpassed nuance from tile to tile. Built of thousands of tiny squares called tesserae, the laid pattern transforms into continuous brush strokes of color, while the tightly packed placement provides structural cohesion.

It is this subtlety of coloration that makes mosaic unique. In a single 12-inch square, for example, each mosaic tile adds its own pattern and hue, varying and deepening the plane.

Mosaic tesserae range in size from 1.5 cm to 3 cm and can be polished, tumbled, or chopped. Most are squares, but rectangles and hexagons are also available. Because the pieces are so small, they can be used to create precise lines, allowing the scale of a design to be changed simply by adding or subtracting a slender row of tiles or by introducing a line in a new color.

These techniques are useful in creating figurative motifs ranging from naturalistically rendered and shaded scenes to geometric borders to textured fields. Many graphic patterns are still drawn from the classical Greco-Roman world where mosaic reached its pinnacle; today's artisans echo the waves, diamonds, keys, and scallops that have been in existence for thousands of years. Add contrasting colors to these motifs, and the flat pattern will acquire a three-dimensional effect. Alter the value range in the palette, and the whole mosaic changes.

Mosaic can also be used to create a solid field of color — a modern choice that works as a highly tactile alternative to a field of ceramic tiles. A single type of stone in repetition will produce a subtle wash of color, while a random combination of stones, either in the same tonal family or from contrasting families, will create a more variegated effect. The particular type of tile fabrication will add to the character of these fields, producing a neat, glamorous feel in polished stone or a more rustic or antiquated texture using tumbled or chopped pieces.

Like any other tile installation, a mosaic is the work of an artist. Expert mosaic artisans achieve balanced color across a field and can make good suggestions about palettes for different graphic motifs. They should be able to lay borders with a continuous corner and, on a broader scale, should be competent to adapt the scale and repetition of any motif so that it fits your particular site. Inspect samples in a showroom or portfolio to get a feel for a mosaic artist's work, and describe your vision if you don't see the exact design you want. Don't reject the possibility of this wonderful decoration even if your job is modest: most mosaicists will accept commissions for projects both large and small.

glass

GLASS IS WATER'S SOLID COUNTERPART. IT IS A TRANSPARENT MEDIUM THROUGH WHICH TRANSFORMATION OCCURS. THROUGH IT WE SEE THE TILE WALLS OF THE SHOWER STALL, THE LANDSCAPE OUTSIDE THE WINDOW, THE COLORED LIQUID IN AN APOTHECARY VESSEL. GLASS IS A FILTER THAT TRANSFIGURES LIGHT INTO DEPTH.

Glass is an affordable material that can be modeled into virtually any shape. As with glazed tile, its surface repels water and is easy to maintain and clean. Glass, like stone, can be fashioned into a mosaic, echoing the luminous depth and saturated color of Byzantine and Venetian tradition, appearing to glow from within.

Glass is used throughout the bath in architectural applications ranging from shelves to shower partitions to tile. Clear glass panes in windows and doors will open a room to natural light. Blown and molded glass provide the bath with an array of beautiful containers to hold the elements of a daily clean routine.

When pigment or a textured film is added, glass can become frosted, translucent, or opaque. When sandblasted, it resembles snowy gauze; or it can be ribbed or etched to achieve pattern. Pearlized glass casts off flashes of violet and ultramarine; milk glass has a cloudy, suspended radiance. Glass can be enigmatic in dark amber, olive, or cobalt — shades traditionally used for bottles, to protect the contents from sun exposure. When glass is laid over a metallic surface, it can also turn prismatic, a fluid, glossy medium for reflection.

translucent

GLASS OBJECTS OF DIVERSE SIZE AND MASS TAKE UP MINIMAL VISUAL SPACE —

With a vast design selection at your disposal, glass and other translucent materials can provide varying levels of opacity to make a "clear" display more dynamic and textural.

an advantage in small bathrooms. This material gives shape to a multitude of vessels that might create an impression of crowding or clutter in denser media. Bowl to bottle, tumbler to tray, squat to lanky, smooth to undulating — the material is eminently flexible.

Glass containers provide elegant storage, exposing only a slender silhouette and the color and texture of the contents: lotions and gels, bath salts, candles, a tumble of soaps. Glass on glass makes possible displays of airy delicacy. And as a neutral medium, it combines superbly with other textured materials.

Still other elements echo the translucence of glass: horn, shell, resin, Lucite, plastic, wafer-thin stone. These materials will enhance an iridescent or monochromatic palette in which glass figures prominently.

the looking glass

The mirror, which is vital for grooming, also reflects and seems to enlarge space. An oversize mirror or a mirrored wall can open up a room and bounce light into dark corners.

The most significant attribute of a mirror is its clarity. A high-traffic working bathroom requires a good-sized flawless mirror for shaving and makeup application, preferably a clean plate of glass with a seamless silvered backing. Old mirrors whose reflective coating has begun to deteriorate and feather should be placed only where they are used as a decoration – in a low-traffic powder room, for example, or as part of a vintage piece of furniture.

You may also want to install a magnifying mirror over the lavatory or in the shower or bath – wherever you focus on skin care, shaving, and beauty routines. These mirrors are wisely placed near a master mirror for a look at the whole face as well as its close-up details.

The best magnifiers use optical glass at a 3x magnification; this gives you a clearer, more precise view than a 5x magnification made with regular mirror glass.

A magnifying mirror can be the flip side of an over-the-lavatory looking glass, it can be mounted on a folding or pivoting arm to one side of the main mirror or on the wall of a shower, or it can be placed on a freestanding easel on the counter or tub deck. It is best installed architecturally at head height, to prevent uncomfortable stooping – a posture that also tends to block the light – and to keep both hands free. Decorative handheld mirrors, traditionally part of antique vanity sets, are useful for checking one's face or hair, but most of them are not true magnifying mirrors.

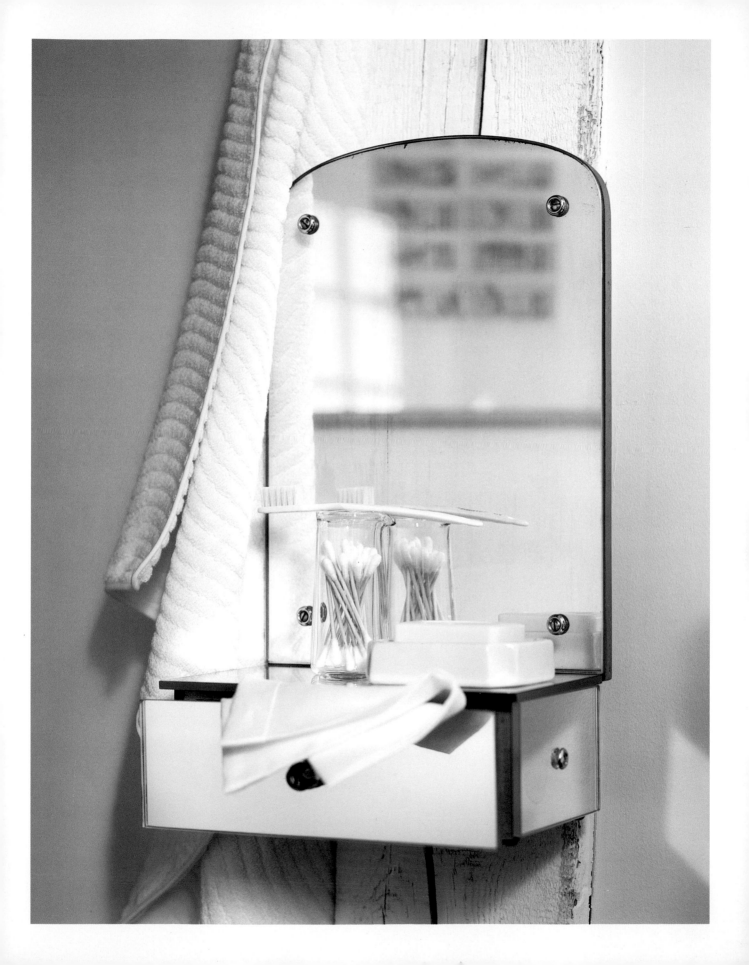

Plastic lacks the luminosity of glass, but for products used in the shower or bath, it is a wiser and safer material to handle. Any bottle that might slide out of a slippery wet hand — shampoo, bath gel, liquid soap — should be made of plastic.

Bubble bath, bath salts, and candles, which are used before getting into the water, can in general remain in glass containers.

plastic versus glass

wood

WOOD IS AS VERSATILE AS CERAMIC IN TERMS OF ITS USEFULNESS AND MALLEABILITY, BUT BECAUSE IT IS DERIVED FROM VERTICAL LOGS, ITS CONSTRUCTION CAN BE FAR BOLDER AND TALLER. IT IS ALSO MORE COLLABORATIVE THAN ANY OTHER RAW MATERIAL IN THE BATH. THROUGH COUNTLESS FINISHES AND CARVED SHAPES, WOOD IS THAT RARE CHAMELEON THAT CAN ENHANCE THE CHARACTER OF VIRTUALLY EVERY OTHER BATH SURFACE.

Because it is porous and vulnerable to water, wood should be used in the bathroom with caution. As a countertop material, wood should be chosen in as wide a plank as possible to avoid seams that can split, leak, and collect dirt. And it is an absolute necessity to seal wood countertops periodically with polyurethane or wax to protect them from water damage. When water stops beading on top of the wood, it is time to reseal the surface.

Flooring especially will warp and erode in a constantly moist room, so wood is best not used underfoot. Dense exotic woods like teak are general exceptions to this rule. In installations where wood floors are a vital element of your vision, take care to keep wet zones like the shower sealed off, protect the tub area with mats, and make sure that ventilation is ample.

Despite its constraints as a surface material, wood is easily employed in the bath as a contextual element. Timbering, wainscoting, and other forms of wood cabinetry and millwork can all bring a distinctive warmth and domesticity to a coolly tiled room. Wood can evoke a natural rustic feel next to terra-cotta or stone; it can also allude to various regional, cultural, and historical styles. When wood is located out of the danger of water, as in most vertical cladding, the chances of damage and debilitation are greatly reduced.

And wood is always welcome as furniture. It has no parallel for creating a classic look, linking the bath to the design ideas long at work in the rest of the home. Secretaries, bookcases, cabinets, tables, chairs, and benches are all pieces that can be imported into the bathroom for display, storage, or seating. And as in other rooms, these pieces can be freestanding or built in, with subtle adjustments of scale to serve the smaller dimensions and lower orientation of the bath environment. Traditional bathing apparatus, like washstands, can also be effective in recalling the furnishing style of earlier bathrooms.

Beadboard walls, old plank floors, and a rustic freestanding cabinet create a warm wood interior for this bath. A departure from protective materials like ceramic and stone, the design is driven by historical mood and seeks consistency with the style and construction of the rest of the house.

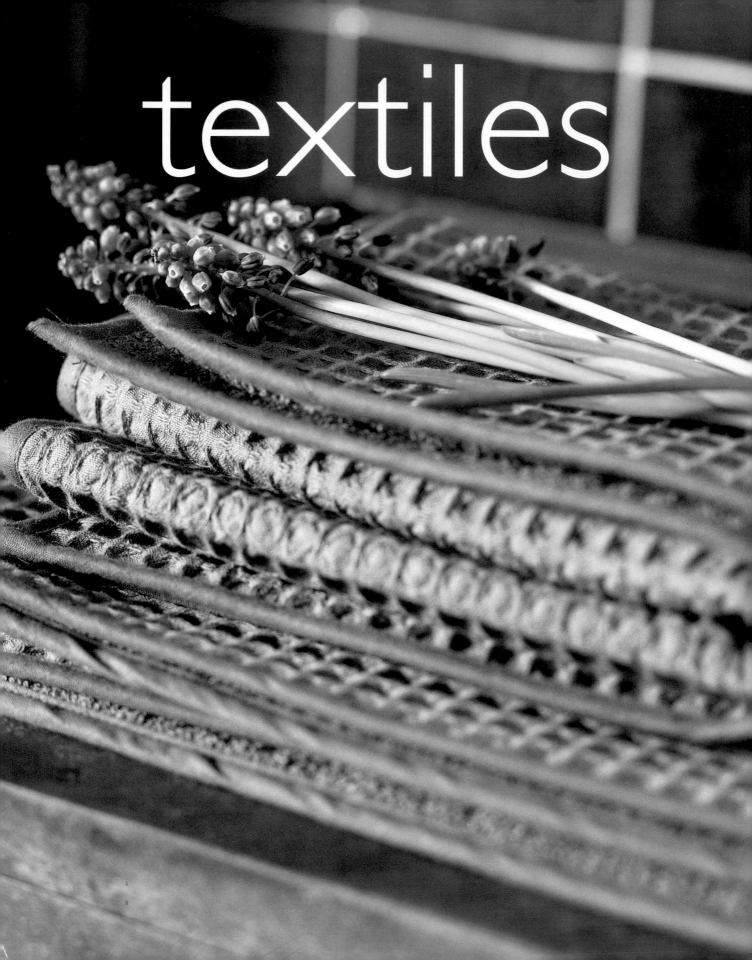

textiles

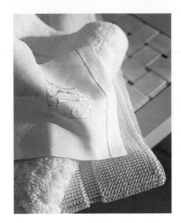

Textiles are the soft refrain to all of the bathroom's core hard materials. They are an integral component to the operation of the space, and they're the items most directly responsible for bodily comfort. As water initiates in the metal pipeline, it terminates in the plush folds of a cotton towel.

Essential textiles include towels in every size for hand, head, and torso; for the bather and the powder room guest. Bath mats and robes will offer further comfort for the wet body, and shower curtains bring a look of drapery into the room.

The principal fibers for all of these applications are cotton and linen, which are inherently absorbent and durable. Spun and looped into fluffy terry cloth, spongy waffle weaves, and classic sheeting, these materials can be dyed a full spectrum of colors or left natural in color; they can be host to a range of textured patterns or express a lavish simplicity with no pattern.

Paramount to any bath textile's performance is the density of its weave, and the length and purity of its fiber. Density is measured in gram weights: a luxury towel will average between 600 and 700 grams. Long staple Egyptian and Turkish cottons, as well as new blends such as pima cotton, yield premium fiber lengths of $1\frac{1}{2}$ to 2 inches. Compare these to the basic American upland cottons used for mass manufacture, which measure only $\frac{5}{8}$ to $1\frac{1}{4}$ inches. Fine cottons have a sumptuous feel, are more absorbent, and last longer than their more modest counterparts.

In the case of terry cloth, which is widely used for robes and towels, the length, or tooth, of each loop, as well as the compactness of loops per square centimeter, will determine the roughness or smoothness of the pile. High-quality terry cloth will have a feathery surface where the ground cloth and the individual loops are not detectable to the bare touch. Velour toweling uses the same pile construction but cuts the loops, producing an equally dense cloth, but with a more velvety texture and a greater brushed sheen. Pile fabrics like these draw water down off the surface of the fabric through each follicle or loop, resulting in a towel that feels dry and warm even as it absorbs water.

More traditional toweling includes linen sheeting and waffle weaves, which are equally thirsty but feel less fleecy. Linen in general is more popular in Europe, where flax has been grown since antiquity. Conversely, cotton is newer and far more popular in the Americas. Improved over the years, washed linen can now be made into towels as supple and downy as those made of cotton, an achievement previously possible only after years of using and laundering this scratchier fiber.

Exfoliating towels with rough, slubbed cotton piles are another recent innovation. And rediscovered hemp is now appearing in the bath in the form of upholstery and shower curtains. This fiber has long been valued for its strength and durability, and it is naturally mildew resistant.

Towel warmers will increase the pleasure of all types of textiles, as well as halve their maintenance: not only will towels remain dry before contact, but they will also dry faster after they get wet — the best protection against mildew and odors between uses.

warmth

Beyond absorbency, the key function of toweling is to warm the body when it comes out of the water and into contact with colder air. Up until that moment, the textile will soak up the condensation and moisture in the atmosphere. This can make any towel feel clammy and cold before it ever makes contact with the skin.

Radiant heat lamps and fans can help keep towels warm and dry during bathing, but heated towel racks represent the best way to accomplish this task. A marvelous luxury for any bathroom, these racks have their own heat source to keep towels toasty and dry. One practical note, however: this installation must be planned in advance of any surfacing installation, as the heating element must be hard-wired into the wall.

In any bath project where extra amenities are a possibility, heated racks are one of the first features to think about. They will increase the pleasure of all types of textiles, as well as halve their maintenance: not only will towels remain dry before contact, but they will also dry faster after they get wet – the best protection against mildew and odors between uses.

apothecary

EDITH MEZARD
eau de linge
lavande

A BATHROOM WOULD NOT BE COMPLETE WITHOUT THE SOAPS, GELS, CREAMS, LOTIONS, FOAMS, SALTS, AND OILS USED TO CLEAN AND TONE THE BODY. THESE PRODUCTS, ALONG WITH THE ITEMS USED TO DISPENSE, APPLY, AND REMOVE THEM – TOOTHBRUSHES, RAZORS, HAIRBRUSHES, SPONGES, AND THE LIKE – MAKE UP THE APOTHECARY SUPPLY OF THE SPACE.

Apothecary preparations have as ancient a legacy as any bathing tradition. Cleopatra bathed in water scented with rose petals to perfume her skin, and she soaked in milk to soften it. In the saunas of Scandinavia, it is a custom to swat the body with aromatic juniper twigs to improve circulation and skin tone; in the Mediterranean, typical formulas for lotions, soaps, and shampoos have for centuries revolved around simple olive oil. In Japan, ground rice has been used for millennia as an exfoliant and is a main ingredient in powder and talcum.

The basic principles of aromatherapy – the use of plants, flowers, and herbs to produce remedial effects on the body – have been passed down through the ages with perfect constancy. The tradition continues through the present: today, advanced dermatological treatments like skin peels and anti-aging serums rely on the benefits of fruit acids and plant-based vitamin compounds.

In an auspicious turn of events, the late twentieth century's revival of interest in the bath has fostered an attendant increase in sensual body treatments and apothecary goods, the majority of which are nature-based. These goods allow even the most modest bathroom to offer a luxurious bathing experience. Anyone who has to save to undertake a major renovation, or who is bound by a restrictive design budget, can still indulge daily in the voluptuous care that fine apothecary products bring to the bath.

Apothecary compounds work on the body in several ways. Through scent, they act on the nervous system to produce invigorating or calming sensations. Through touch, they invite a nearly unconscious massage that benefits circulation. Through chemistry, they strip dirt and oil from skin and hair and seal water in. The essential oils and stimulating enzymes in a plant extract like eucalyptus, mint, ginger, or citrus will open the nasal passages and create a tingle in the skin; relaxing products containing chamomile, calendula, or lavender soothe the senses and have a calming, anti-inflammatory effect on the skin.

Soap is at the center of any bathing tradition and is used at every fixture. The finest milk-, honey-, and olive oil–based soaps derive from French and Italian traditions dating back to the Renaissance, when monastic orders of herbalists began standardizing recipes for body treatments to serve royal patrons. Today these ingredients, as well as other vegetable oils, including coconut and almond, continue to be prized for their gentleness and moisturizing properties; as a result, as much olive oil goes into soap production in Italy as into culinary products.

At their best these soaps are triple-milled for density, producing bars that last a long time and hold their shape as they shrink with use. Most examples are opaque and can be perfumed with a limitless number of scents. In a direct reflection of their ingredients, pure olive oil soaps are usually green; other bases produce a wider range of pale shades. Clear glycerin soaps are a newer introduction that lather exceptionally well but don't hold their shape or last as long as milled varieties.

The bar of soap remains an object of familiar custom in the bath, though now it appears in a wide variety of sizes, from huge shower bricks to small guest lozenges. When selecting soap, it is wise to try out the bar in hand first and make sure it fits comfortably. A form too big will be difficult to lather evenly, while conversely, a bar too small for its intended location and traffic load will disappear too quickly. Bars used in the shower will melt faster than those by the lavatory or bathtub. Surveying personal issues of use will help you choose appropriate shapes and forms for each fixture in the room.

Liquid soaps and gels are another option that removes constraints of size as well as the imperfect look of a dwindling bar. These products usually come in packaging that remains stable for the life of the product. Bottles can be very decorative or simple and label-less, suggesting a bath's private stock that can be refilled whenever the contents run low.

Wrapped, unwrapped, or assembled in combination, soap is one of the daily visual pleasures of the bathroom. Available in every conceivable size, color, shape, and scent, soap bridges beauty and utility.

Ceramic tile is the most common and rich surfacing material for the bathroom. It is the rudiment with a thousand faces, inextricably bound up with the long history of bathroom decor.

From the ancient traditions of Byzantium to the diverse ethnic legacies of Morocco and Spain, Portugal, Italy, and Holland, tile has always been a medium of cultural expression as well as a valued building material. White tile suggests the medicinal purity of the great nineteenth-century European spas; elaborately patterned tile evokes the mystical opulence of Moorish palaces or the exotic inlaid embellishment of the Turks. Bright-colored majolica tile suggests a lush Mediterranean villa or a sunny hacienda in Mexico drenched in blue and yellow.

Victorian, Art Deco, and Arts and Crafts tiles are available for every kind of architectural project: curvilinear reliefs in subtle colors, romantic transfer-printed botanicals drawn with a naturalistic line, bold shapes painted in dense, complex glazes. These tiles echo the design of the late nineteenth and early twentieth centuries, when handcrafted furnishings still prevailed over a growing number of homogenous mass-produced products for the home. With a renewed devotion to craftsmanship, contemporary tile artisans are bringing a fresh eye to the discipline, exploring new mediums — encaustics, metallic pigments, ingrained textures — as well as nontraditional styles of surface painting.

Tile is still used generously in the modern home — in kitchens, across fireplace mantels, on exterior walls, and in courtyards; beyond these applications, however, the material at its essence connotes bathing. Tile's form-fitting hand-laid surface has long represented the most efficient construction method for managing moisture and heat. And because of the sanded grout that holds it in place, tile's gridlike topography actually provides traction, making it the best defense against dangerous falls on surfaces slicked with water.

The current renaissance in bathroom design has resulted in a wider range of tile textures and colors than ever before. Top-quality handmade tile is now making a comeback and can elevate a bathroom to an extraordinary level of sophistication. Celebrated reissues and renewed production by many famous American studios of the 1920s, '30s, and '40s indicate a strong return to handmade designer tile. Yet beyond type, it is the visual interplay of tone, pattern, and texture — properties embodied in every kind of tile — that validates this medium as a decorative force. For decades tile choices in this country were slim and unexciting, but tile is once again being recognized as a premium design element.

{exploring} tile

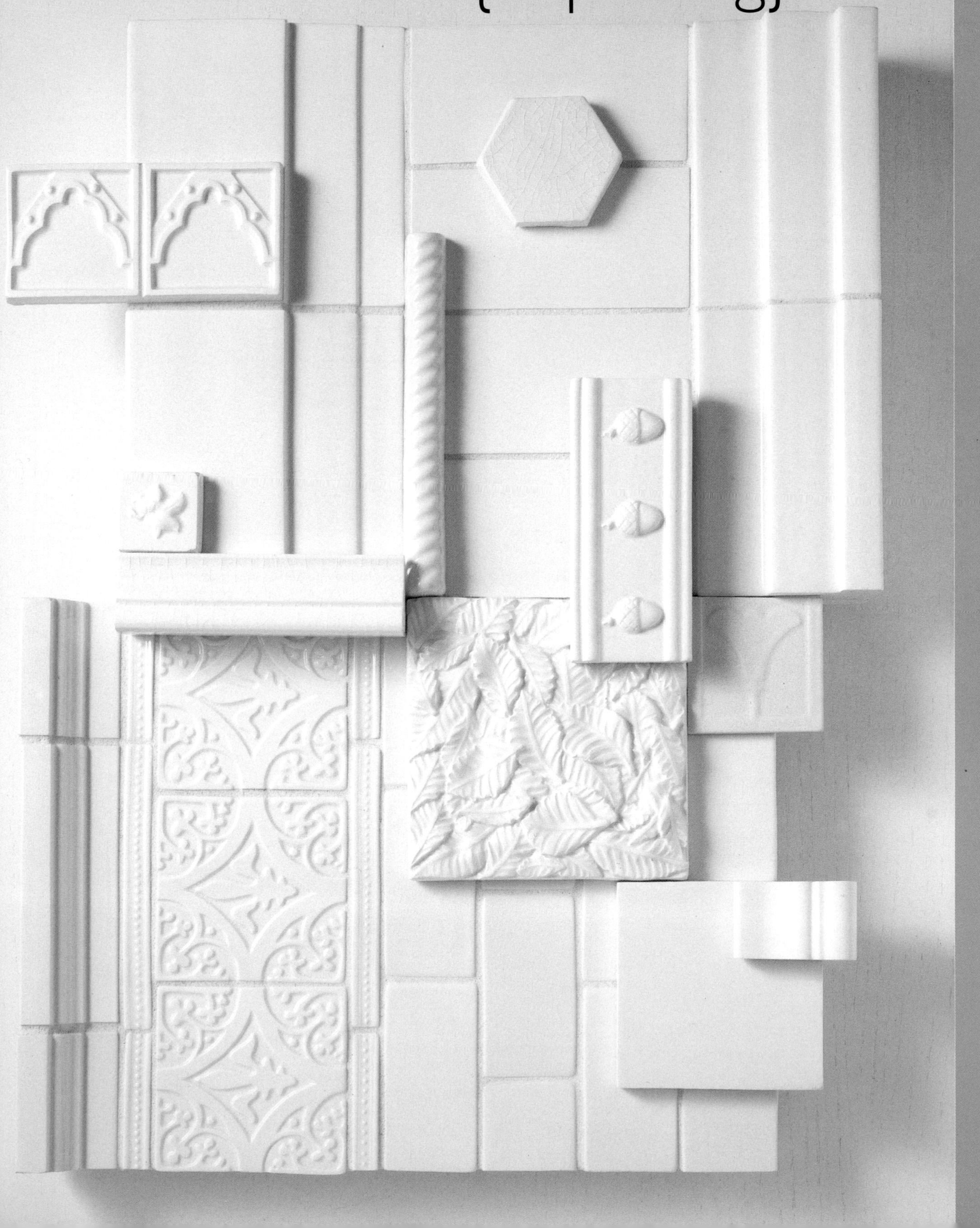

By definition, tile is any modular element that is organized in a grid to produce a comprehensive surface. Tile can be made of stone, glass, ceramic, wood, cork, linoleum, or any other material that fits into a grid.

Because of its flexible manufacture and architectural strength, ceramic is the most developed of these materials. Ceramic tile thus encompasses the most numerous designs. Pieces fall into four overlapping categories: field tile, finishing tile, transitional tile, and decorative tile. These classifications apply to handmade as well as manufactured examples. All ceramic tiles are clad in a permanent glaze, which protects the clay body and gives the tile its color and design. A glaze is any glass compound colored with metal oxide that bonds chemically to the clay or bisque when fired. The glaze, combined with the shape, helps to determine the use of each type of tile.

As a rule, families of ceramic tiles will encompass all of the elements mentioned at the right. In combination, they can produce a cohesive, complete installation. Tile design is purely subjective, however, and creative exceptions to any standard abound. For example, offset field tiles in a contrasting color, size, or pattern can be used as borders or decorations. A patchwork of decorative tiles in a contained area, like a splashboard behind a lavatory, can equally determine the surrounding choice of field tile instead of the other way around. Patterned layouts — like pinwheels or herringbone grids — can also work as designs within the field and will provide a generalized effect of texture.

The usefulness of tile on floors, walls, and outdoor areas depends on its strength and temperature resistance. The method of application is determined by the density and type of the bisque, the nature of the surface glaze, and the duration of the firing. It is important to select the appropriate tile for each aspect of a job: using a fragile decorative tile underfoot, for example, can result in a cracked and unstable floor surface.

Tiles come in standard weights, providing the right ceramic grade for each type of installation. Before you select your tiles, consult with a knowledgeable salesperson to make sure that each style fits its setting.

finishing tiles

comprise moldings and base pieces that cover architectural planes. Other elements such as stop-ends, returns, bull-noses, outside frame corners, and quarter rounds are made to serve a specific purpose, and help to cap a field with a finished edge.

liners, or transitional tiles

include thin or wide decorative pieces that break the field and create transitions To other tile phases. These pieces are usually called liners. Liners can be selected in contrasting colors or in monochromes that blend with the field. They may be simple and utilitarian or extremely detailed.

decorative tiles

may be highly ornamental and are best used to build a motif that relates to the field. Taking their cues from fine art, they often have allegorical, architectural, or botanical themes. The designs may be black-lined, as in stained glass, sculpted, painted, or transfer-printed.

field tiles

are the basic square, rectangular, or polygonal components that cover walls and floors. They are usually a solid color and at best should have some tonal depth or texture. Patterns that can be used over wide expanses are called textured fields.

{exploring} tile

HANDMADE TILE

Handmade tile is of special value in creating a satisfying ceramic landscape. With limitless variations in glaze and hue — no two pieces are ever alike — handmade tile lends subtle modulation and flowing movement to any static plane. Just as different shades of green make up a meadow, so do the distinctions from tile to tile dissolve into a sweeping whole, producing a dimensional surface.

Glaze is the secret of this medium and the source of its uncommon splendor. The way it pools, puddles, and falls off the edges of each piece, as well as how it reflects light and shadow, gives the field a depth and tonality unlike that of any other material. Even in the palest hues, the effect is of liquid strokes of color. Far more than manufactured tile or flat paint, the nature of handcrafted glaze will make a surface come alive and vibrate with texture from every angle in the room.

Each batch of handmade tile is unique. Every studio uses different clay and additives, which determine the personality of the raw body — its bisque, color, texture, and modeled shape. Glaze recipes and techniques are often closely guarded to prevent imitation.

The firing of the glaze further multiplies the variation. Different glazing methods produce distinct and unpredictable effects of texture, color, shading, pooling, and crackling. Finishes can run the spectrum from glossy to matte.

Other circumstances account for each tile's one-of-a-kind appearance: the method, time, and place of firing all have an impact on the way a glaze finally sets. No finish, even within the same batch, can ever be exactly duplicated.

AFFORDING TILE

Tile is often the element that sets the tone for the entire bathroom. For this reason it should be of the highest quality you can afford throughout your installation.

Handmade tile is typically more costly than manufactured tile, but it doesn't need to upset your budget for the entire project. For example, in a 40-square-foot space, for under two thousand dollars you can purchase enough handmade tile to wainscot the walls and surface the floors.

That expense will increase or decrease depending on the number of specialty pieces you use, versus simple field tile. You can combine a number of handmade decorative tiles with good-quality mass-produced field tiles. In general, however, the seamless depth and texture in a handcrafted field will be more rewarding (and less dissonant) than small quantities of fancy tile punctuating a generic surface.

The hidden expense in tiling is the installation, and that aspect of the job relates to handmade and manufactured elements alike. Tile setting, however, is an art form that is worth paying for — talented installers are valuable collaborators who bring a trained eye for proportion and balance to the physical layout of a tile design and who know how to set a clean, tight, consistent grid that won't detract from the sweep of color or pattern in the overall surface. A good tile artisan will love and respect the material as much as you do and will make valuable suggestions about how to center a design for symmetry in the room, as well as how to best finish edges and corners.

Always factor the price of a skilled installer into the total cost of your tile, so that you aren't caught with empty pockets when the job is under way. Integrate this sum into your budget to make sure it doesn't drain funds earmarked for other parts of the project.

TILE DESIGN

Tile is an architectural material, so it's important to determine your choices early on in the design process or in conjunction with choosing the major furnishings. It is especially helpful to coordinate this material with the finishes of your metal fittings and other surfacing materials.

Focusing first on field tile will help to develop the mood of a space. The overall texture and color of a modeled field will create the strongest visual impact, so this is the easiest element to start with.

Identify what you like about the color and feel of individual tiles; then consult sample boards to see what the tile looks like in repetition. Notice the difference in the character of a tile once it's part of a group. Is the color more intense? Is the texture neutral or primary?

Think about how a field color or texture will look when it's installed over a large surface. Imagine how the pattern and sizes of tiles can produce a dynamic, cohesive background all on their own.

Err on the side of neutrals. Tile is an affixed construction that will last for decades, so it is prudent to approach color choices with an eye toward moderate, natural, and clear hues.

Where possible, choose finishing and decorative elements from the same family of colors and textures as the field tile. This uniformity will reduce the risk of inconsistency and will prevent the look of different artists at work on the same canvas.

With handmade tile especially, take care to review and approve the quality of the batch before installation begins. You should buy more tiles than you'll need, so that you will have a wide range of pieces to compose with as well as some extras if tiles break. Don't be alarmed by the tiles' natural irregularity; glazes can be unpredictable and will take to each surface slightly differently. Even the simplest all-white design will show beautiful depth and variation; that's part of the material's charm.

At home, lay out some of the tile to get a feel for its shadings and subtleties. With handmade tiles, move individual pieces around until you achieve a smooth brush stroke of color with an even distribution of dark and light pieces. Plot out any decorative elements and set up the finishing tile to harmonize with the field. Select the grout color that best matches the overall layout.

Make sure that you or your designer is present when installation begins, so that the tile setter understands your vision. You will live with the result for years, so be prepared to take responsibility for the design — grids and grout lines included.

Tile installation is permanent. Careful planning at the outset will help ensure a pattern that is complete, balanced, and clean.

part 4

principles

ARBORS & TRELLISES, BREEZ
FENCES & GATES, S

HAWKINS and ABBE

VAN NOSTRAN

MARTIN **Fences, Gates and Bri** RACTICAL MANUAL HOOD

IN ANY ARTISTIC DISCIPLINE, THE MOMENT

WHEN A DESIGN BECOMES A PHYSICAL REALITY IS THE MOMENT THAT MUST PIT WHAT

A THING *IS* AGAINST THE VISION OF WHAT IT *COULD BE*. IT IS THE FINAL STAGE IN THE

LONG WINNOWING PROCESS OF CREATION, A FUNNEL FED BY INTENSE STUDY, ANALY-

SIS, IMPROVISATION, AND TECHNICAL PREPARATION THAT YIELDS AT THE END ONE

VERY SPECIFIC RESULT. IT IS THE PRINTED TAKE BEFORE THE CAMERA, THE FINAL CUT

AND FIT OF A SUIT, THE DECISIVE NOTE COMMITTED TO THE SCALE.

What all these acts have in common is a commitment to choices. As the design process moves forward, each round of decisions becomes more limited and concrete, culminating in the leanest, most accurate representation of what the artist has in mind. And the more work that gets done ahead of time, the easier it is to arrive at a holistic and inspired final product.

In the bathroom, this means taking time to evaluate different materials and equipment. It also means working through the functional requirements of the room on paper until the whole space – structure and infrastructure – comes together into a cohesive and workable plan. As you approach the actual installation, it means that energy (and a portion of the budget) should be spent identifying a team of skilled consultants and artist-craftsmen to set the tile and stone, do the architectural drafting, and provide whatever services you can't complete yourself.

Putting this groundwork in place before purchasing a single item will do much to avert crises of budget, performance, and style once the installation is under way. This way you can avoid dead ends and wrong turns so that the working blueprint will be reliable, realistic, and approximate to what the space will look like when it's built out. The planning process is akin to an artist's sketching an image before moving to the final canvas; then drawing a guiding outline, only at the last to be fleshed out with paint.

At this point, intuition and taste take over to give a design its particular life. This process constitutes the interaction of color, pattern, texture, and scale, basic organizing principles that are at work in every aesthetic composition. The way these tools are ordered and exploited creates endless variation within any drawn template. The same fundamental floor plan assumes a very different look, for example, when outfitted with color-washed tile rather than dense stone, or with a freestanding tub instead of a deck installation. Inherent in these choices are priorities of solidity versus line, detail versus mass – preferences based on creative instinct as much as educated judgment.

Because the bath should ultimately be an artistic as well as a practical environment, it makes sense to learn how to use the artist's principles, recognizing them in various materials, controlling their impact when they're combined in different sequences, sculpting with metal, painting with tile. They constitute the room's palette; they are the language that creates specificity at the point where the dream gives way to the draft and the draft gives way to the finished product.

color

COLOR IS A MECHANISM FOR CREATING THE VISCERAL MOOD AND FEEL OF AN ENVIRONMENT. LIKE ANY TONAL LANDSCAPE – THE EXPLOSION OF PRIMARY HUES IN A SPRING GARDEN, THE SHADOWY STEEL OF CITIES, THE BLEACHED AND LUMINOUS TINTS OF THE SEASIDE – AN INTERIOR WILL REGISTER INSTANTLY AND AS A WHOLE IN TERMS OF COLOR. MORE THAN JUST A SURFACE EXPERIENCE, COLOR EVOKES A TOTAL BODILY SENSATION.

The most livable colors tend to have direct elemental counterparts, so an effective way to work with color is to select a palette that suggests an authentic natural landscape. Color is a significant concern in the typically small environs of the bath, where its appearance in structural materials is permanent. The goal is to create a quiet, holistic backdrop rather than a loud, synthetic veneer that is distracting or trendy.

Choosing color is an emotional undertaking. One person may favor layers of it in vivid shades while another is inclined toward the most transparent expression of materials in their natural state. Follow your instincts. Take note of repeated colors in your wardrobe or the furnishings in other rooms of your home, and use those as guidelines. Your own preferences are the best barometer for the lasting satisfaction of any palette.

neutrals

BECAUSE MOST OF THE BATHROOM'S FIXTURES ARE WHITE,

neutrals work well here and appear to extend organically from white. Earth tones communicate a simple, textural, and classic look, while the addition of tonal shadings in brown, ivory, ocher, khaki, or gray will give the space an understated richness and will help avoid a clinical monotone.

Neutrals can exist anywhere on the spectrum from cool to warm and can incorporate strong hues as well as pale washes. Even a solid field of dense color can work as a neutral if there is minimal color imposed around it.

Soft colors in shades of stone, bark, moss, heather, sand, and linen attract light and keep a room looking airy and tranquil; intense colors born of earth, air, fire, and water will enclose the space, creating a cocooned atmosphere. Deeper greens, reds, and blues, as well as mineral tones, befit this latter approach, and work as allusions to grass, leaves, soil, sea, and sky.

Walls, cabinetry, and accessories blend into an enveloping palette of creams and taupes in this simple bath. The controlled color range, at work throughout the room, allows each individual hue and material to register clearly yet read as part of a serene whole.

tone-on-tone

A LIMITED PALETTE COMPOSED OF LIGHTER AND DARKER SHADES

of the same color will create texture and dimension, and can unify disparate elements in a space. Tone-on-tone color can bring order to a varied assortment of materials such as marble, porcelain, wood, tile, metal, and linen. It can also add character to rooms with very moderate or simple elements, enlarge small spaces, and highlight intimate details and architectural flourishes – a beautiful crown molding perhaps, or a slender ribbon of tile. Using shades of a neutral color or of white, tone-on-tone creates an elegant, recessive interior that permits greater focus on pattern, texture, silhouette, or proportion.

bold

STRONG SATURATED COLOR BRINGS RICHNESS AND INDIVIDUALITY

to a bath interior. It is the most explicit way to announce the mood of a space and to suggest a cultural reference – the jewel tones of India, or the bottom-less reds of China, or the intense primary colors of Pop Art.

While pale and neutral colors help to conceal architectural flaws and imbalances of scale or silhouette, bold shades tend to cast a space and its contents into high relief. Whether cool or warm, bold colors can effectively emphasize the smallness of a room, playing it up rather than attempting to obscure its limitations. In the same way, they also help to humanize large rooms by creating an enclosed feeling. This occurs because color has a visual density that not only holds the eye but creates the illusion of space advancing toward it – an optical trick that allows intense color to gain primacy over other decorative motifs.

In bathrooms where the fixtures are unassuming, bold colors can provide a spectacular backdrop. These colors can also be employed sparingly, either in paint or in textiles and furnishings, as punctuation to a scheme where other types of sculptural or plastic effects are featured.

As a rule, the stronger the color, the more dominant it will be in an overall design. For this reason, solid expanses of bold color work best where they won't compete with overt elements of pattern. Shades should be selected for depth and texture, and even primary colors should be toned up or down so they don't appear flat – a particular caution in children's bathrooms where fundamental colors are easily outgrown. A good test for any bold shade is to check it against the intensity of color in a mineral like lapis, cobalt, or cadmium. To have durability, the tone should be penetrating, not flat.

contrast

COLOR CAN BE USED TO CREATE PATTERN

by combining contrasting shades. In small touches, polarities of color can highlight dramatic details, delineate positive and negative fields, and produce graphic motifs. In broader strokes, they give a room a layered feel and flatten dimensional surfaces.

Strong contrasting colors are a staple of many decorative folk traditions, from Morocco and Mexico to India and Italy, especially in tile. Tile is perhaps the most common arena for exercises in contrast and color; but textiles, carpets, and painted surfaces provide other outlets for this ornamental style.

Contrast is often at work in geometric fields, where solid blocks of color combine to produce a variety of design grids. In these configurations, bright hues are well paired with soft neutrals in order to relieve the eye over broad expanses. The most classic contrast, black and white, is an archetype of continental decoration and has the greatest impact in terms of motif and mood. Married evenly in a simple checkerboard, arrayed rhythmically in an intricate lattice, or brought in to accent other colors or each other, black and white suggest urbanity and bring a sleek visual wit to the bathroom.

Vibrating graphic stripes appear to push the walls outward in this small bathroom. The white-on-white installation looks especially crisp against the polarized texture of the walls; the elliptical bands echo the proportions of the subway tile below in a subtle visual harmony.

White is an umbrella color that defines the style and pristine constitution of most modern bathrooms. Consider its ubiquity: fixtures of hard white china; snowy white cotton swabs and toilet paper; opaline bath milk, soap, and salts; downy cotton robes and towels. White speaks of something intangibly clean. It is the pure partner to clear light, glass, and water.

Because it is visually so immaculate, white provides a unique psychological comfort in a room designed for doing away with dirt. More than any other color or element, white remains lofty and cloudlike, the color of vapor made solid. It is always a step removed from earth and ore.

White also suits the practical operation of the bathroom better than any other color, since it can stand up to detergents and bleach with no loss of pigment. But though it is sterile in function, white never needs to be sterile in look. When treated as a color, as opposed to an absence of color, it offers an incalculable range and depth; it can accommodate infinite degrees of shading and adjust to the hue of any other color. It can run the spectrum from stark to lush, cool to warm, dense to sheer, bright to ombré, hard to soft. The nuances are often so subtle that any number of shades of white will register to the passing eye simply as white; variations become apparent only when samples are lined up next to each other for comparison.

Do this kind of comparison to determine preferences of tone and to ensure that the whites you choose will suit the other colors in the room. Look at a wide range of whites to assess whether you are drawn to shades scored with blue, red, or yellow or whether you favor whites that veer into beige, khaki, ivory, or gray. Blue-whites are compatible with chrome and stainless steel, for example; warmer amber-whites best suit nickel, brass, and lumin; and rosy or lavender whites will pair well with silver. Take care also to investigate which white blends with a particular shade of marble or ceramic tile; verify that other paints originate in the same color family or a complementary family. Specify water-white glass, from which the natural greenish oxides have been extracted, if you want a transparent or soft white palette.

If you plan to focus on white as the chief or only color in a design, diversity of hue and finish will make all the difference between a flat space and a dynamic one. You can achieve white-on-white by repeating one basic value in a mix of diverse materials or by juxtaposing shades of white in related finishes and mediums. White is also an excellent color for modeled effects, especially in ceramic tile, where the variation can come from subtleties of glaze as well as from relief or extrusion techniques. Like glass, white straddles the domains of color and texture, allowing for numerous overlays of surface pattern without losing its weightless quality.

Following the principles of a tone-on-tone palette, the white-on-white bathroom can yield a timeless, understated look that will have great longevity. Its paleness will help to open up space and reflect rather than absorb light, producing an expansive, awakening effect in environments of any scale or style. It marries beautifully to other light-casting materials like metal and glass — absolutes of every bathroom — and retains an enveloping clarity in denser mediums like fiber, ceramic, and stone.

Because it's easy to maintain in the clean space of the bathroom (impractical though it is in other rooms), white appears in products for this environment with more sophistication and variety than any other color. Take advantage of this in your selection of towels and accessories, and the white profile of the bath will be transformed into a robust, personal space that never feels medicinal or cold.

{exploring} white

pattern

PATTERN IS A STRATEGIC DESIGN DISCIPLINE THAT WORKS IN PARTNERSHIP WITH THE MORE EPHEMERAL, EMOTIONAL NOTION OF COLOR. IT IS THE PLAN BY WHICH ANY THREE-DIMENSIONAL PLANE OR COMBINATION OF PLANES IS PLOTTED FOR DYNAMICS, RHYTHM, AND ATTITUDE, USING A SEQUENCE OF LINEAR SHAPES AND/OR THREE-DIMENSIONAL MOTIFS TO ENLIVEN A STATIC GROUND. IT CAN BE INHERENT IN A MATERIAL OR DERIVE FROM THE INTEGRATION OF DIFFERENT MATERIALS; IT CAN RELATE TO THE ARRANGEMENT OF SHAPES IN SPACE OR DETERMINE THE DIMENSIONAL EFFECT OF A FLAT SPACE, SUCH AS A GRID OF TILE.

In all its forms, pattern is a product of contrast, a juxtaposition of one material, color, or shape next to another to create a kind of sensory punctuation. Expressed in the bath primarily through surfacing and especially through tile, these contrasts can delineate the various architectural regions and planes of the room.

Because it is related to surfacing, pattern must be considered in many key structural decisions: identifying ratios of width, breadth, and depth between elements; scaling the repeat of the pattern to fit a space; lining up a field with the center of the room; deciding where to place fixtures; or choosing the best material to achieve the desired design. Executing a pattern is significantly technical, so methods of setting benefit appreciably from the input of a skilled installer. The best tools to guide this process are deceptively simple – a level, a ruler, and patience – but they must be in the hands of an artist as well as a technician: make sure your installer is both.

A grid of cubicles lends order and balance to the freestyle pattern of towels within. Piles are rolled and stacked in different formations to counter the geometry of the frame, adding rhythm to the repetition.

Pattern is made up of two components: the motif in each building block of a design, and the larger motif generated by combining those building blocks in repetition. These two components can be assembled in various ways; it is the choice of material that is crucial to the resulting design. For example, materials with natural irregularity like stone, wood, and hand-glazed ceramic tile will yield patterns with *implicit* texture, while more regular surfaces like paint, glass tile, some types of factory tile, resins, and polished cement will produce patterns with a smoother *explicit* texture.

In considering pattern, follow the same instincts that inform selections of color. If you favor bold motifs, look for explicit textures; if you like subdued patterns, choose implicit textures. There is no right way to sort through the options, but color and pattern are so interdependent that it is important to link one set of preferences to the other. Inverse relationships tend to prevail here: pale, neutral, or tone-on-tone colors make room for richer and more layered expressions of pattern, while strong, saturated, high-contrast colors work better with figurative or recessive patterns.

grids

Square grids can range in size and diameter from the diminutive 1–3 cm of mosaic tesserae to 24-by-24-inch stone pavers and beyond. In between are all the standard dimensions of ceramic tile. Wall grids tend to use tiles that are anywhere from 1 to 8 square inches. Floors start at 2 square inches and go up to 24 by 24 inches.

Changing the proportions or orientation of the checkerboard will produce grids with diagonal, rectangular, polygonal, and compound profiles. These formats are typically aided by tiles in the shape of rectangles and hexagons, which are available in standard sizes. Squares turned on their sides become diamonds. These basic tile shapes, joined by triangles and octagons, can be assembled in a vast number of ways to produce complex decorative grids and borders. Such patterns are traditionally used for floor designs rather than walls.

Grids are graphic plates that produce the core repeat of any pattern. They are made up of organizing units such as tiles, planks, or stenciled figures that are assembled into a cohesive motif. Grid formats are almost always present in the bathroom, and virtually every type of building material can be fashioned into grid cells.

The basic grid is a square checkerboard or lattice where horizontal and vertical axes cross in equidistant spacing. This format is the foundation of all tiled motifs. Wood and other rectilinear components used in paneling, wainscoting, and flooring are organized along parallel axis grids and result in a striped or grooved rather than a latticed motif. Stripes tend to produce a sole elongating effect on space, while diagonal and lattice grids can create both expansive and compressive effects, depending on the way their scale relates to the environment.

Many of these grids make use of a technique called *offsetting,* in which the seams of any tile or plank are staggered by row, as in brick bond. This method invests a pattern with a subtle but crucial rhythm, depth, and movement, and helps to manage components of different shapes and sizes in combination, such as moldings, caps, and liners set against a field.

A clean, level grid is in many ways more difficult to achieve than an offset one, because inconsistent measurements or spacing from row to row can throw off the harmony of an entire field. If the grid is uneven in any swath, the eye will automatically gravitate to the inconsistency – the place where the grout line has swayed or where the field ends abruptly. Using offset grids will help to avoid these problems and will in general mask the imperfections that are common to virtually every surface installation.

Tiled grids offer the greatest safety benefits for flooring because the sanded grout used between the tiles provides traction for wet feet. For this reason, they are a must for shower stalls and are a good choice for bathrooms used by children and the elderly. Small grids – say, 2- and 3-square-inch ceramic tile or mosaics – with a lot of grout are good choices for these installations, and also work well in large bathrooms where the pacing between fixtures leaves stretches of floor to cover on bare feet.

In any flooring pattern, the greatest precaution to take for safety is to lay down bath mats around each fixture. Textiles offer the soundest traction on hard flooring that is slick when wet; slippers are another good safety measure.

Floors can effectively be clad in any type of surfacing material. Large flagstones and pillowed terra-cotta tiles create an expansive outdoor feel because they are often adapted from wider-scale exterior paved areas. Tiles of this dimension are best used in spaces where there is room to repeat the pattern.

A gridless or seamless field is also a possibility. This produces a very modern, spare, and clean-lined environment in glass, plaster, marble slab, poured cement, terrazzo, or molded resin, all of which can be discharged in large expanses. These materials are best specified in honed, pitted, tumbled, troweled, or granulated finishes that offer a rudimentary amount of traction.

This small-scale octagonal mosaic offers ideal grip for a floor surface destined to be wet and slippery. Radiant heat installed beneath the flooring helps to evaporate water quickly and enhances comfort underfoot, especially in cold weather months.

flooring

field

The pattern within a grid can be geometric or organic, orderly or random, symmetrical or diffuse. These effects may derive purely from contrasts in shape, size, and direction, as in a herringbone or basket weave grid, or they can be achieved through contrasts in tile color or material, as in a variegated mosaic or a stone floor with ceramic tile inserts.

With a monochromatic palette, pattern will result from the outline, or negative field, in which the tiles sit — namely the demarcation of grout seams. This effect produces a neutral, recessive texture that sweeps across the eye.

Where contrasts between mixed colors or materials are used to define the pattern, as opposed to a linear grid, the design becomes a positive field. Any positive field will seem to advance toward the eye, and so stake the foreground in a decoration. Materials that work well with this technique include black-and-white tile and multicolored marble inlays. Color blocking can also energize a positive field in effects that range from amorphous tonal washes to asymmetrically patterned Mondrianesque graphs.

In both positive and negative fields, grout is best applied in a light, coordinating value that allows the pattern to read within a crisp frame. Fine grout seams should fall within a range of $\frac{1}{2}$ inch to $\frac{1}{16}$ inch, making them as slender and nondisruptive to the surface as possible. These measurements are as applicable to the irregularities of handmade tile and certain stone floors as to machine-made or gauged materials. It is a common mistake to pad extra grout around tiles with erratic edges or thickness; this will magnify rather than downplay imperfections in the grid.

Spanning from floor to ceiling, this unusual square brick bond field produces a very clean, continuous canvas that recedes behind the major fixtures and opens up the space. In such broad swaths, the tile functions as an architectural skin rather than a decorative element.

In tiled surfaces, the pattern carried by individual components is frequently used to enhance a simple grid. Such patterns can be reserved for periodic appearances, as decorative breaks in a field, or they can be applied in repetition to create a lively field.

Such patterns can come from an inherent variation in a natural material like stone, but most derive from applied surfaces. This type of pattern usually results from the manipulation of a raw medium like ceramic, glass, plaster, wood, or metal during its fabrication, yielding varied types of reliefs with both visual and physical depth.

Applied surfaces can be either two- or three-dimensional. Sculpting and extrusion (the process of squeezing material through a relief mold) build pattern above the surface; incising and etching embed pattern in or below the surface. Glazing and color washing create a modeled pattern through painterly layers of pigment; transfer printing, silk screening, and stenciling convey linear pattern onto a negative or positive background. Pressing and molding create extremely regular textural patterns like ribbing. Parquetry and inlay render graphic pattern with a strong illusion of shading and depth.

applied surface

Applied surface pattern represents one good way to link a bath installation to the decorative tenor of other interiors. Although color in the bathroom tends to be emphatic and is not obliged to echo the palette of the wider home, applied designs can execute in microcosm the look that one prefers in a general environment. These surfaces are the place to mimic the loose pattern carriers that give other interiors their texture and life – tableware, bedding, textiles, artifacts, books – all within an affixed matrix that conforms to the regimen of a wet space.

ARCHITECTONIC TILE

Architectonic tile is a type of applied surface, but it moves beyond traditional tiled designs to create a new kind of pattern and symmetry for an interior. Rather than being assembled through repetition of a grid, which produces either scenic or textural imagery, this tile uses systematic blocks to build an extended architectural motif. The effect is global to the room, with a sequential composition that captures the rhythm and diversity of classic architectural decoration – the art of ceramic applied to the techniques of millwork and masonry.

Architectonic tile is ideal for highlighting or creating structural features in a bath, as one would do in any other room of the home: developing the intersecting planes of the wall and ceiling with an articulated molding, raising the edge of the floor with a foundational plinth; building out columns, paneling, and wainscoting; framing mirrors, lighting sconces, and showerheads with a decorative surround. Repeated and coordinated motifs promote ease of installation; in the case of some of the bath's standard features, prescaled kits, including all the necessary framing elements, simplify the installation even further. Different styles derive from a range of architectural orders, including Federal and Palladian, Classical and Neoclassical, Modern and Chinoiserie. Beyond transcending the square block of tile, pieces can vary in shape and character from reeding and beadboard to flutes, serpentines, and guilloches; from rosettes to annulets, Greek key liners, and bamboo reliefs.

As a means of paneling, this category offers an entirely new approach to patterned field tiles. Examples include foliated wreaths and swags, stippled paint stripes, chip-carved textures, plus and minus blocks, and Chinese fretworks – modular designs that can be assembled into larger motifs over extended stretches of wall. These fields, interspersed with any number of frames, liners, and other transitional elements, produce a crisp geometry and dimension in a room whose walls are flat and peripheral.

All these types of tile have the delicacy and detail of milled woodwork, with a regularity that makes them effortless to assemble, and a nuance of form and line that gives them lasting character. Adapting the qualities of ceramic glaze to this type of surfacing produces an extraordinary depth and fluidity of shading, with tonal palettes in graded ranges of dark to light shades that unify the overall landscape. The effect can be one of bold, subtle, or monochromatic color, with high definition accents or quiet, low-contrast shifts from one detail to another.

The patterns in architectonic tile can vary to suit the size and significance of a given site. Large rooms can absorb a good deal of architectural detail, whereas small rooms that might be overpowered by an elaborate design scheme can still benefit from fine details. Take care to relate the amount of tile to the scale of the raw surroundings, and let architectonics give a space decorative importance and stylistic credibility.

rhythm

Rhythm is one result of pattern. As in music, it is the syncopation of different components in a design blending together, creating a spatial cadence that gives an installation movement and dimension. It is the product of repetition and coordination, both within a single pattern and bridging different patterns.

Rhythm may be either symmetrical or asymmetrical. Symmetry in general produces a classical effect, though it should always derive some movement from varied or implicitly textured materials. Asymmetry, with its roots in Art Deco and midcentury architectural themes, evokes a modern design approach. In these types of decoration, the materials should be crisp and simple, letting the collusion of shapes form their own textured rhythm — oddly measured paces, elongated and compressed silhouettes, field dimensions that fall outside of perfect one-to-one or one-to-two proportions. Very often an awkward or irregular floor plan can be turned into a design asset by playing up its asymmetry; in the same way, a blank, boxy room can be visually enlarged when clothed in an asymmetrical pattern.

In all patterns, rhythm is made of colors and shapes applied in mathematical ratios. It is the practice of gradation, where solid block forms trade weight with silhouette lines, where rectilinear shapes play against curvilinear, and vice versa, all within the dilation of a beat — the repetition in a grid. A rhythm's density or lightness, tightness or looseness, depends on the nature and dimension of that basic pattern. As a general rule, the larger and more monochromatic the pattern, the more relaxed the rhythm.

In some situations, fixtures can serve as elements of rhythm themselves. Doubling certain furnishings — two basins in a console, two freestanding pedestal lavatories, two mirrors instead of one panoramic plate, a water closet paired with a bidet — can produce a strong visual tempo.

Rhythm also guides the relationship between foreground and background in a pattern. In a coherent rhythm, only one element at a time should seize the foreground, while other parts of the design form a tonal surround behind it. Too many components competing for attention at once, or at the same volume in every part of a space, will spoil a rhythm and create a cluttered, dissonant, or muddy installation. This is one reason why simple white fixtures with good mass are so advantageous in the bath: they offset the intricacies of pattern in a floor, wall, or surfaced countertop; and they will act as a neutral backdrop for the rhythm of textiles, accessories, and fittings displayed around them.

Architectural framing can also perform this role — for example, repeating inset coves for both the water closet and the shower stall. When large forms such as these appear as vehicles of rhythm, they read as extremely prominent visual solos that are best supported by minimal or implicit patterns in the background.

texture

Texture is the skin possessed by every material, color, and pattern in a design. Like rhythm, it works both in detail and as a whole, aggregating into the sum *feel* of a landscape: it is germinal, describing an initial tactile response to each surface, and it is gestural, mapping the overall flow of surface. Texture operates on both a visual and a physical level of perception; it is appearance and sensation combined.

A texture can look smooth and feel smooth, like glass or porcelain, or it can have a compound effect, looking and feeling different. Think of highly grained marble or wood, or a clear jar revealing a tumble of bath salts: these materials appear complex and patterned to the eye, but they feel polished and sleek to the touch.

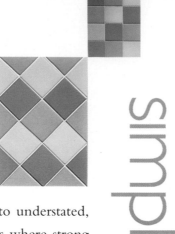

Simple textures lend themselves well to understated, minimal, and classic American interiors where strong sculptural shapes and colors hold the focus. The best materials to use in such rooms are glass, ceramic, plaster, paint (on walls and wood furnishings), lacquer, and textiles with a buff, combed sheen. Polished metal furniture and cement surfaces push the room toward a unisex or masculine style and give it an industrial look, a popular choice for bathrooms today.

Compound textures make pattern a sensory priority in a design. By their nature they play with illusion, so they represent a good way to enliven unremarkable architecture and manipulate depth and width in spaces with undesirable scale. For example, compound textures can produce an enveloping effect in large, open rooms that might otherwise feel drafty, or they can suggest spaciousness in small rooms. They can also be used as punctuation to draw the eye to particular details in a multizoned space.

compound

layered eclectic

Layered textures throughout a room produce a nineteenth-century Continental decoration, as well as popular international folk styles such as those of Morocco, Spain, Mexico, the Middle East, and Turkey, all regions with elaborate tile traditions. Patterned tiles and architectonic field tiles work well in these styles. Other good choices are figured rather than solid textiles and naturally textured materials like wood, stone, mosaic, and weathered metals – all dispensed in lavish amounts.

More recent design approaches combine compound and simple surfaces to create eclectic textures. These types of decoration juxtapose concentrations of pattern with stretches of clean space, creating a frame for unusual admixtures of old and new pieces, and a fresh context for fine furniture. The effect is modern without being stark, and historical without being cluttered or plainly literal – a promising new direction for the bath that most instinctively echoes the furnishing style at work in the rest of the home.

surface

Certain textures, in any installation, will work together better than others. Plain, reflective surfaces and light colors work well in repetition; they also relieve the eye when used as accents in darker or patterned palettes.

via a dynamic mix of surfaces. Your goal with surface is to create a pleasing rhythm and balance, yet preserve the crispness and interest of each material.

The fail-safe mechanism in this process is the layout of the room, which maintains its own texture loop. Surfaces that interact with the naked body, like countertops and fixtures, should be smooth, while the need for traction demands textured floors. The hard core of the installation can be softened with towels, robes, shower curtains, and bath mats. Slick metal fittings provide a contrast to wall and floor grids. The room will be well balanced as long as appropriate materials are used for each basic function.

Following this template, you can plot the combination of materials for your installation — simple or compound, layered or eclectic. This advice applies to every step of bath design, from new construction to renovation to overlay decoration.

In this process, it is useful to look at nonbathroom interiors, fine art, and even automobiles and fashion rather than other bathrooms as sources of inspiration. You will get a better instinctive gauge on what you like and don't like if you view tubs, showers, tile, and faucets in a broader design context.

Next, gather samples of different materials and look at them in combination. Also take time to view model vignettes in bath and tile showrooms, where articles are arranged together to highlight medleys of texture. See which polarity a palette is leaning toward, and adjust the colors, patterns, and shapes in your own scheme accordingly. Try to see where each material belongs in a general spectrum: cool-to-warm and light-to-dark for color; textured-to-plain for pattern; mass-to-line for shape. This will leave you with fewer details to compare.

As you begin to collect surfaces, keep in mind that highly textured materials like wood, stone, and cloth, as well as richer colors, work better in combination than individually. Wood on wood, for example, may lose depth and focus if the masses start to blend together without crisp outlines, but wood on ceramic, glass, or stone will preserve the distinct edge of each material. Tile on tile and stone on stone work when differentials of scale, shape, and color are employed, but any combination looks better when the primary material is joined by contrasting toweling and accessories.

If a room revolves around a large architectural or decorative element, like a curving wall or a grand vintage fixture, it's best to choose a smooth, plain texture rather than an overt pattern. Smooth textures will highlight the physical contours of the form, whereas a pattern will draw the eye inward, away from the silhouette.

light

polarities

All textures operate in yin and yang: rustic-refined, cool-warm, smooth-rough, intricate-plain, bold-subdued, sleek-distressed, organic-mechanical. A majority of textures that swing toward common polarities – cool-sleek, bold-mechanical – will produce a discrete tonal range or rhythm. Conversely, a juxtaposing of opposable textures – any two halves of a pair, dense terra-cotta and weightless glass – will create a stronger, more sculptural dynamic.

Polarity makes the difference between low-contrast and high-contrast decoration. If you favor designs with tonal sweeps of pattern and color, you should select a palette with minimal polarity – a marble bathroom with white or neutral furnishings, for example. Or if you like high-definition motifs with overlapping lines, patterns, and colors, combine polarized elements to dramatize the setting: the same marble bathroom with dark wood furnishings.

play off certain surfaces to produce shifting modes of texture. Wind creates a momentary ripple in flat fabrics; air and water over time will cause metal, paint, and enamel to oxidize and patinate. Water in the tub will form a tidal landscape, changing white porcelain to a cellophane green-blue, erupting in foam with the addition of bubble bath. But on a daily basis, no agent is more influential than light, which can transform surfaces from shiny to matte, bleached to dark.

Smooth, polished, glassy surfaces deflect light. Grooved, worn, etched, or ground surfaces absorb and diffuse it. To bolster the effect of light in a dark room, choose materials that are smooth and reflective; to create a warming effect in a cold or floodlit room, opt for materials with a matte texture or pure color.

In the first stages of a design project, take into account the quality and amount of natural light a room receives. If that light is abundant, be aware that temporal and seasonal shifts from bright morning light in spring and summer to ombré evening light in fall and winter can utterly change the complexion of the room and produce fluid shifts in the texture of virtually any material and color. In rooms with little or no direct light, this flickering radiance can be imitated by reflective materials – tile, polished metal and stone, mirrors, glass accessories, and high-gloss paint and plaster – especially on large surfaces. Use candlelight and ambient light along with your basic task lighting to create glow and shadow.

The best bulbs to use around vanity and grooming mirrors are halogen, which imitate clear natural light. Mirrors are the one place where you should always strive for transparent and stable light, so that you can accurately see skin tone and, for shaving, whisker direction. In addition, basic overhead lights will pitch shadows over the face at a mirror, so it's always wise to add light covers or sconces on either side of the glass to correct the glare.

A crosscurrent of natural light assures bright illumination for this attic bathroom, minimizing the need for ambient or overhead room lights. Sconces on either side of the mirror remain a must, day or night, providing directed task lighting for grooming.

scale

SCALE GOVERNS THE ORGANIZATION OF OBJECTS IN A SPACE, AS WELL AS THE DIMENSION AND BALANCE OF EACH SHAPE. IT IS BOTH A TECHNICAL AND AN INTUITIVE DECISION, USING MEASUREMENT AS ITS LANGUAGE, AND THE ART OF PLACEMENT AS ITS MUSE.

A well-scaled space produces a feeling of well-being and comfort, whereas if the scale is out of balance, a sense of awkwardness and disharmony will prevail that no amount of craftsmanship or sheer material beauty can undo. In this way, scale can create environmental poise or destroy a design despite the most discriminating outlay of materials. An error of just half an inch in the placement of handles on a deck can throw off the proportions of an elegant lavatory or bathtub; a fixture too big or small for its surroundings can dash the scale of an entire room.

physical scale

Certain problems of scale can be resolved with common sense–for example, making sure that the body will have sufficient space in the room and that each fixture will suit the body. These questions of physical scale and fundamental usefulness can be answered by simply walking through a showroom or site and trying out several fixtures. Are the elements oriented, especially in a small or vintage bathroom, so that there is sufficient clearance between fixtures, walls, and doors? Is the showerhead high enough? Is the tub long and wide enough? Is the lavatory bowl deep enough? Have counters and decks been installed at an appropriate height?

Prior to any discussion of design, you should go through this type of physical checklist. It is a good test for decisions that will affect the comforts of your bath routine. It will also help you avoid repeating the awkward proportions of older bathrooms, in which many postwar fixtures, and all vintage fixtures, were designed for smaller people. Today's manufacturers have begun to increase the scale of their products so that there is a good deal more variety and flexibility in the basic apparatus than ever before.

proportion

IN BOTH TWO- AND THREE-DIMENSIONAL DESIGN,

the most aesthetically satisfying proportions follow the golden mean, which is defined as the division of a line so that the shorter part is to the longer as the longer is to the whole (approximately 8 to 13). You can discover golden mean proportions in virtually every type of art, and they are the basis for both traditional composition and modern asymmetrical design. Yet because this balance is so programmed into the way we see and move through space, pleasing proportions are created by intuitive judgment as often as by strict calculation. This is the alchemy of scale, the ability to eyeball a form and sense how much of one shape or color belongs next to another.

Proportion is expressed in every object and surface in the bathroom. It also operates in the way those elements are brought together; again, the relationship of the part to the whole is key. And so the same rules prevail: fixtures and furnishings that are proportionate to the architectural frame produce a tranquil, classical symmetry and reveal the true dimensions of a room; elements that are disproportionate to the dimensions of a space are far more common, and offer a key way to manipulate perceptions of scale and room size.

Effects of proportion and symmetry can be achieved with disparate materials and shapes. Here three individual elements – mirror, lavatory, and cabinet – are lined up along a median vertical axis, uniting the overall composition into a rectangle that aligns with the height and width of the setting.

illusion

(imagine the rabbit-hole chambers of *Alice in Wonderland*); but at its best and most controlled, it can create an illusion that will redirect the visual layout of a room. Good devices include the use of inverse proportions: bringing big elements into a small space and small elements to a big space. In all rooms, an expanse of space will amplify the aura and scale of individual furnishings.

Diagonal grids will make a room feel larger, as the pattern will appear to run on a longer bias. Grids with white or light-colored tiles will suggest depth, appearing to push back walls and make floors wider. Floor grids that are smaller than wall grids also amplify a room's height and width: the bolder walls appear to expand outward and upward from a receding ground. Paneled grids like wainscoting inflate the vertical elevation, especially when they break at overscale heights. A large grid or seamless field of stone that covers an entire wall can also suggest height in a low-ceilinged room.

The same scale grid wrapping around from floor to wall, as with field mosaic or stone slab, will make an installation read as one large container with softened corners that give a cocooned feeling. And small grids will preserve the scale of a small space, as they form a continuous texture that is soothing to the eye and does not call attention to itself.

Impressive horizontal or vertical axes in a room can also be accentuated by dropping furnishings out of symmetry with the space. These arrangements produce surprises based on distortions or collisions of scale. In a room with unbroken panoramic lines, a console can be overscaled to span a wall, or a single washstand can be positioned off center, leaving a large run of space on one side. In a bathroom with a high ceiling, a low-slung tub might be set before a soaring bank of windows, or a marble shower stall might be clad up to a high molding with a low splash wall faced in the same stone in front of it. In each case the interior volume of the fixture remains static, while the surrounding architecture grows keener and more electric.

Juxtaposing a tall narrow cupboard against a low water closet creates an illusion of height in this space. The parallel planks of the cupboard reinforce the vertical orientation and loom larger than the wainscoting behind, playing also with perceptions of depth.

overscaling

Forms designed on a larger than standard scale produce a general association with modern design and capture in particular the bold American architecture of the 1920s and 1930s – the age of the great skyscrapers; the power of industry and big machines.

Because of these industrial references – visions of gears, steel, chrome; the sleek aerodynamics of cars and trains and monolithic towers – overscale objects are ideally suited in the bath to work through metal: fittings and their accessories, washstand bases, furniture. Outsize accessories are especially suitable to this style, with retro towel racks, soap dishes, shelves, sconces, hooks, bath caddies, toothbrush holders, and mirrors that have changed little in profile since the days of luxury bathrooms in such grand Art Deco hotels as New York's Waldorf-Astoria, or London's Claridge's or Savoy, or in the baronial mansions of America's Railroad Age. This aesthetic also carries over into more contemporary and minimal designs, with a focus on clean, unadulterated lines and a scale generous enough to hold masses of plush towels and artful collections of apothecary products.

In a larger room, amplified forms and masses will take precedence over smaller-scale patterns, emphasizing a strong sculptural shape in lieu of more delicate linear ornament. Following this principle, bathrooms that are chiefly fixtural in design, with limited palettes, minimal pattern, and few accoutrements on display, will appear overscale even if the basic forms are not. There is less in the landscape to attract the eye, so the perspective expands; each major element seems to be farther from the next in the vacant surround.

fit

FIT WORKS IN EVERY JOINT WHERE INDEPENDENT ELEMENTS MEET.

Set against the panorama of a double window, this tub station fits its site perfectly and positions the bather to enjoy the view. Towels, robe, and accoutrements are all within arm's reach, outfitting the experience for total convenience.

This can mean anything from the grout seams in a field of tile to the way discrete parts of a faucet or a valve are assembled (mechanical fit); the tight seal between a fitting and a deck (structural fit); the way the body folds into a fixture (physical fit); or the dynamics of adjacent materials, patterns, and colors (aesthetic fit). In this range of applications, fit is the line, either transparent or explicit, that relates one form to another. If those relationships are balanced and taut, the fit is successful. If they collide or are sloppy, the fit fails and the system breaks down.

Expanding on this definition, fit is also integral to the placement of furnishings and objects in an overall space (environmental fit). This is where fit is a reaction of scale, matching the dimensions of a floor plan to the placement, size, and shape of the elements that go into it.

In outfitting your bathroom, remember that intimate spaces are as valuable as an abundance of space. While bathrooms with large dimensions are an obvious luxury, for the purposes of the bathing routine they may be overpowering or lacking in privacy, making the user feel exposed. Keeping in mind that a normal body temperature of 98 degrees is at least 4 degrees cooler than a hot shower (a really hot shower can creep up to 106 degrees), you can see that your bathroom will benefit from enclosed areas that hold warmth and protect you from cold air and drafts.

A good way to manage large spaces for warmth is to break the floor plan into smaller zones — the lavatory area, the tub or shower area, and so on. These zones can be separated by half-walls, screens, and scrims, or doors made of translucent glass, all of which will preserve privacy in a communal space like a family bath. A small separate room for the water closet, following the European tradition, is also becoming increasingly popular in America today.

In a more casual approach, all areas can be arranged in an open plan, each anchored by its fixture like a sculptural piece of furniture, with different surfacing materials or changes in grid pattern demarking the shift from region to region. For example, tile can be used to frame the perimeter of a shower stall, create a splash deck around a lavatory, or form a carpetlike platform beneath a tub, leaving the field between elements and on walls to create cohesion in the overall space.

Perhaps the most central detail of environmental fit is the placement of towel bars close to each water source. No bath is fitted correctly if you have to walk across the room to collect your robe or a towel. This fundamental detail is often overlooked in the rush to present towels as objects of display. Freestanding pieces like a tiered rack or a small table laid with hand towels can work well in an open-plan approach and may help to produce a dynamic interior rhythm where not every furnishing is fixed to a wall.

In small rooms where towel bars must go up on walls, take care to map their placement in correlation to the surface grid so that they are installed with the least possible visual interruption. In general terms, this means knowing the scale, shape, and location of all architectural accessories before a single surfacing tile is installed.

character

A BATH INSTALLATION IS LAUNCHED UPON A THOUSAND DETAILS OF TECHNIQUE AND STRUCTURE. IT IS DESIGNED WITH HUNDREDS MORE DECISIONS AND DOUBTS, FALSE STARTS AND URGENT SPRINTS. COUNTLESS HOURS ARE SPENT SEARCHING, BROWSING IN SHOWROOMS, PORING OVER BOOKS AND MAGAZINES, DIVIDING BUDGETS, AND MULTIPLYING SQUARE FEET. EVERY DECISION IS PERMANENT. SO MUCH DEPENDS ON MAKING WISE CHOICES.

And then, out of some deep instinct, suddenly answers arise: here is the color that feels right; here is the bathtub I want to lie in; here is the soap that smells like summer; here is the fitting made for my hand. At these moments the project becomes a room again, a place that is manageable and tactile, conducive to reverie, sprung from reason.

Creating this space is ultimately about bringing such sensibilities into the equation and remembering that each element of the room is chiefly at your disposal to bring you comfort. The noble lavatory with its contoured lines is an inert object until you turn on its faucet; the towel has no purpose until you fold yourself into it. The installation does not come alive until it is inhabited, in rhythms so simple that complexities of design begin to ebb out of mind. And so a hand reaches for a vial of bubble bath; toes tickle the steaming surface of the bathwater. The lights are turned low, candles lit. The bathroom derives its character from the felicity of these smallest details as much as from the composed landscape they sit in.

In this most intimate space you can celebrate your own routine. The bathroom is a cultivated interior deserving of care and decoration, but it is also a private place in which to be naked and under no scrutiny but your own. Sing in the shower. Dream in the bath. Splash in the water. Get wet.

Procedures Prior to Starting Your Bathroom Project

Discuss your needs, preferences, and dreams for your new bathroom and clearly communicate them to your designer or architect.

Prioritize and then decide where you will compromise.

Go to a well-designed showroom with professional sales associates who can help you make educated decisions about the products you will need.

- Try out all of the products that you anticipate using.

- Use your sense of touch for the products that interest you.

After you have made your product selections, meet with your architect or designer and together discuss space planning.

Review all drawings for spatial accuracy, proportion, scale, and fit.

When your drawings are complete, you are ready to competitively bid the project to contractors.

Select your contractor carefully.

- Ask to see examples of his work.

- Make certain that the jobs you inspect relate to the type of project you anticipate doing.

Check tile installations for grout joints and tile cuts.

Check walls for their smooth finish.

Check plumbing for alignment and clean installations.

Check all millwork for construction details and finish.

Inspect finished painted surfaces.

- Communicate with his references.

Ask detailed questions regarding his work habits.

Inquire about the subcontractors.

Set a realistic construction schedule with appropriate penalties for work that extends beyond the agreed time frame.

Check the work each day.

Establish a good working relationship with the contractor so that he communicates with you.

Mother Nature Does Not Make Dye Lots

Variations in color tones, crystalline composition, veining, and mineral activity are characteristic and to be expected.

Samples cannot indicate what an entire order will look like; they are only representative of the general nature of that stone type.

Stone is often packaged in Styrofoam boxes, and it is wet when packed, so it will look darker. Pull several pieces from the box and let them air dry to check the color.

Procedures Prior to Installation

"Dry lay" the stone.

- Take several pieces from six different boxes.

- Mix the stone on the floor, looking for a blend of the color range.

- Blend the variation until you get a sense of the palette.

- Communicate your preferences clearly to your carefully selected contractor.

- Protect your newly installed stone from dirt and other abuse during construction with paper or masonite.

- All extra stone should be labeled and saved for any future repairs.

- Stone is naturally porous and needs to be protected against daily dirt and staining.

- Sealing procedures are a necessary part of the installation process.

- Prior to grouting, a coat of porous plus sealer must be applied.

- After the grout has been installed, another coat of porous plus must be applied.

- Stone needs regular maintenance. Frequency of future coats of sealer is dependent on the use of the space. It is important to use the products recommended by your professional sales associate or installer.

- Stone, like other natural products, will age. This will only add to its inherent beauty.

Fittings are the hardware of the bathroom. They control the water flow. Fittings include tub mixers, shower systems, and faucets.

Lavatory Fittings

are used to mix hot and cold water and direct it into the lavatory bowl. The rough plumbing is concealed below the lavatory deck.

Shower System Fittings

Exposed Shower Systems consist of components in which the rough plumbing is visible but plated and incorporated into the finished bodies. The plated rough plumbing is then mounted externally on the finished shower walls.

Concealed Shower The volume is controlled by the on/off valve.

Thermostatic Mixers allow the bather to select the water temperature. The internal mechanism will maintain this selected temperature at all times.

Pressure Balance Valves maintain a set temperature by adjusting the flow of water in response to fluctuations caused, for example, by toilets flushing or by washing machines being activated.

Showerheads disperse water for showering. The size of the heads and the patterns of spray vary with the type of head selected and the amount of water pressure delivered to the head from the shower valve.

Handshowers are showerheads attached to the wall with a hook or cradle. Exposed hoses hang on a shower wall. They are useful for hair washing, baby bathing, and cleaning the tub or shower.

Body Sprays are small heads mounted on the vertical shower walls to spray an intense jet of water directly at the user's upper, middle, or lower body, depending on placement. Usually they are used in pairs or threes.

Spray Bars are vertical bars mounted on a shower wall. Multiple small openings on each single bar provide intense sprays of water at the user's body.

Tub Filler
This fitting mixes hot and cold water, sending it into the bathtub via the spout.

Exposed Tub and Shower Mixer
This tub filler is either deck mounted on pillars, wall-mounted, or installed on freestanding exposed legs, with a diverter that is concealed within the finished body. The hot and cold water are mixed within the body and diverted to either the spout or the hand shower. The hand shower is mounted on a cradle on top of the mixing body.

Deck Set – Concealed Tub Mixer with Hand Shower
This deck-mounted filler has a connected hand shower, with the rough plumbing connected below the tub deck. The hot and cold water are mixed in rough plumbing and spilled out of the spout or diverted either by a diverter built into the spout or mounted on the deck through the hand shower.

Tub Spout
This fitting is used to deliver water into a bathtub; it must be connected to, or be an intrinsic part of, a mixing system.

Bath Rack
A metal framework that supports itself by resting its rubber-coated arms on the tub rim. It is used for holding soaps, sponges, and other bath items. Bath racks may be available with a mirror or book stand.

Corner Basket
A triangular wire structure available in different sizes to be mounted in the corner of the tub or shower area.

Double Towel Bar
Similar to a single towel bar, this has two rails supported by end brackets with supports for both rods. One rod projects out farther than the other.

Freestanding Mirrors
Freestanding mirrors can be two-sided, offering magnification on one side and a standard mirror on the other. Useful for placement on a dressing table or vanity.

Freestanding Soap Holder
A two-piece unit consisting of a base, which is cast brass and plated, with a porcelain dish insert. The dish is easily removed for cleaning.

Freestanding Toothbrush Holder
A base and a plated brass frame that stands alone and holds toothbrushes.

Freestanding Towel Rack
A decorative cast-metal structure that stands alone, has rails at different heights, and is used for hanging towels.

Paper Holders
A roller supported by brackets, which holds and dispenses toilet tissue. This roller can be a spring-type, or it can be L-shaped, allowing the paper to slide over it. Freestanding models are available.

Robe Hook
A hook mounted on the wall or back of a door and used for hanging robes.

Shower Seat
A small bench with wall-mounted chrome support brackets. The seat folds down for use in the shower and flips up against the wall when not in use. The mounting must be done with proper blocking in the wall.

Single Shelf
A single piece of glass supported by a pair of brackets and mounted to the wall. Typically placed above a sink, it is intended to hold small bath items.

Single Towel Bar
A towel bar consists of two wall-mounted end brackets and a porcelain, crystal, glass, or plated brass rod. The bar is available in various lengths and holds one or more towels.

Soap and Sponge Basket
A rectangular wire structure, larger than a soap or sponge basket, that has sections for soap, sponges, and other bathing items. The basket is mounted to the wall in the tub or shower.

Soap Basket
A wire basket mounted to the wall in the tub or shower and used to hold soap or sponges.

Three-Tier Shelf
Three shelves supported by a framed bracket.

Towel Rack
A wall-mounted storage unit consisting of a shelf and a towel bar and used for storing as well as hanging towels.

Towel Ring
A metal or porcelain ring on a bracket attached to the wall, used to hang hand towels.

Towel Warmer
A multitiered towel bar with a small heating element to warm bath towels.

Tumbler Holder
A wall-mounted support for one or two tumblers.

Wall-Mounted Mirrors
Mirrors can be two-sided: one side has a standard mirror and the flip side has a magnifying mirror. Wall-mounted mirrors are available in a range of shapes and sizes. The extension mirrors are used for close-range tasks, like shaving and putting on makeup.

Chrome
This hard plated surface is durable and resistant to stains and scratches. A universal finish that is compatible from manufacturer to manufacturer.

Nickel
A softer, warmer, and rosier surface than chrome. Nickel from most manufacturers is compatible. Care must be taken to maintain this finish with a soft cloth and nonabrasive cleaners.

Lumin
A brass-colored product, plated with a gold-and-nickel alloy that makes it tarnish-resistant. Each manufacturer uses a slightly different formula to achieve this finish, so colors are not compatible. This product needs to be wiped dry with a soft cloth to prevent water spotting.

Unlacquered Brass
This natural polished brass will tarnish over time. The finish can be repolished with a mild agent.

Matte
A soft and uniform metal surface achieved by brushing heavily coated polished nickel with a wheel to which mild abrasives have been applied.

Backsplash
The wall area, usually 18 inches high, between a countertop and the bottom of the kitchen cabinets; or the wall area, usually 4 to 6 inches high, between the countertop and the bottom of an inset bathroom mirror.

Bisque
Tile that has been fired but not glazed; also, the fired tile underneath a glaze. Sometimes called biscuit.

Cement Backer Board
A manufactured subsurface that is nailed or screwed into place for the adhesion of tile and stones.

Ceramic
Fired clay or a mixture of clay and other inorganic material, either glazed or unglazed.

Clay
A mixture of kaolin (aluminum silicate), quartz (sand), and traces of minerals such as iron and feldspar, which is plastic when wet. Ceramic tiles are made of clay.

Crazing/Crackle
A characteristic of many translucent glazes, fine, hairline cracks in a glaze intentionally created by the tile manufacturer simulate an aged effect. All crackle tiles need to be sealed.

Curing
Process during which a new tile installation is allowed to set. For unglazed tiles, curing must occur prior to sealing.

Expansion Joint
A joint filled with flexible material that can expand or contract slightly without cracking the surrounding tile. Usually applicable for commercial projects.

Extruding
Squeezing wet clay through a die to form variously shaped tiles, most commonly moldings.

Glaze
A glass compound colored with metal oxide that bonds chemically to the clay or bisque when fired.

Glossy Surface
A very shiny surface that reflects light.

Grout
A cement-based filler for the spaces between installed tiles, terra-cottas, and stones. Grout is available sanded and nonsanded and with many additives. Your tile installer should be the expert on the latest technological advances in grout production. Epoxy-based grouts are also available.

Kiln
An oven used for firing ceramic tile.

Light Traffic
A term generally applied to residential interior light traffic floors. Bathrooms are generally considered light-traffic rooms.

Membrane
A layer of sheeting that separates the backing surface from the mortar to protect a tiled shower floor from water, cracks, and instability. Also known as a cleavage membrane, or a moisture barrier.

Mitered
Cut on an angle to meet an adjacent tile.

Mortar
A tile-setting medium that is applied in a malleable wet form, which hardens to bond tiles to a surface.

Mud-set
A mixture of cement, sand, and water in specific parts to be used as a bed on floors for tile. Mud-setting is the preferred method when a subfloor needs to be leveled or when tile is either ungauged or has an unstable backing.

Pillowed
Tile with a slightly rounded surface, like a flattened pillow.

Porous
Permeable, or absorbent. Porous surfaces need to be sealed to make them impervious to water and other matter.

Relief
A sculptured surface, usually produced by pressing clay into a mold.

Satin Glaze
A semi-matte glaze that reflects more light than a true matte glaze.

Terra-cotta
Natural clay taken directly from the ground or mixed with other clays, then dried and fired.

Thin-set
An installation setting bed, usually $\frac{1}{8}$ to $\frac{1}{4}$ inch thick and consisting of a mixed powder of dry sand, cement, and additives to which water is added. Can be used for most flooring installations of ceramic tile or stone when the subfloor is stable and level, like most cement slabs, or when tile or stone is all the same thickness.

Wet Saw
An easy-to-use tool for cutting ceramic, stone, terra-cotta, and some glass tiles. A rotating diamond-blade saw is cooled by a water bath; the water also keeps the tile cool during the cutting process.

The following names and descriptions are intended to standardize our tile language. This should facilitate ordering, choosing, and selling tile. Please note that not all pieces are available from all manufacturers. Some pieces might be available only in certain forms and not in others, even if they are from the same manufacturer.

Bullnose
Field tile with one rounded edge and a flat back. Used in thin-set installations to finish off an area of field tile when no molding is being used. When using rectangular tile specify if long or short side is to have a bullnose edge.

Double Bullnose
Field tile with two adjacent, rounded edges and a flat back. Allows the bullnose to "go around the corner" and connect a vertical edge to a horizontal one. Used to finish off an area of field without a molding. Made for thin-set installations, it is also called a down angle.

Jam Bullnose
Field tile with two rounded edges on opposite sides. Used to create shower curbs and shower door surrounds. When ordering rectangular pieces, specify if the long or short side is to have a bullnose edge.

Mud Cap
Functions like a bullnose except that it accommodates full mud installation and creates a 90-degree return to the wall.

Mud Down Angle
Functions like a double bullnose but is used in full mud installations.

Mud Base
Also called a sanitary base, it creates a curved transition from floor to wall. Best used when wall and floor tile are of similar thickness. The top edge can be straight-cut to accept field tile above it, or it can be fully finished and used like a wooden baseboard.

Quarter Round
Allows two edges of field tile to meet at the outside corner of a wall while creating a rounded 90-degree return.

Cove
Opposite of a quarter round, a cove creates a rounded inside corner at the junction of two field tile edges.

V-Cap
Used on counter edges and tub decks, the leg, or horizontal extension, allows the piece to hang on the top of the counter for added support.

V-Cap, No Leg
V-cap with the horizontal extension removed so that it can be used as a rail molding.

V-Cap, Outside Corner
Wraps a V-cap around a 90-degree corner with the same support advantage of a regular V-cap. Creates a smooth and safe edge.

Miter Corner
Cut on the job by skilled tile setters, this is the easiest, most flexible way to wrap a molding or liner around an inside corner.

Rail Molding
Used to cap an area of tile wainscoting, either by itself or in combination with a decorative border. Smaller ones can be used to frame mirrors.

Filled and Glazed End
Allows a run of molding to stop with a straight blunt end that is fully glazed. Needed only when working with moldings that have hollow cavities in back.

Stop End
Creates a finished end to a run of molding at an outside corner while providing a cover for the molding that meets it. Better and safer than an outside miter-cut end, it provides flexibility if the wall corners are out of square.

Outside Corner
Like a V-cap corner, but this is a rail molding piece that wraps around a 90-degree outside wall corner without the use of a miter cut.

Frame Corner
Used to carry a molding around the corners of a mirror or an opening, such as a doorway. The thinnest or flattest section will be toward the inside.

Reverse Frame Corner
Same as a frame corner except that the thinnest, flattest section is toward the outside edge.

Crown Molding
A decorative molding that joins the wall to the ceiling.

Liner
A plain linear piece intended to have tile or trim above and below it.

Border
A decorative band intended to have trim or tile above and below it.

Base
Usually set on top of the floor, base acts just like a wooden baseboard to finish the bottom of a wall. Sometimes called skirting.

Deco
A piece of field-size tile with an impressed or painted decoration on its face.

Splash
Similar to a V-cap except that the horizontal leg is shorter than the vertical one. Used in mud installations to finish the top edge of a backsplash.

architectonics terms

Annulet
A ring-like design motif. When a series of such rings overlap or intertwine, the resulting pattern is called an annulet interlace.

Astragal
A molding that when viewed in section, is perfectly symmetrical. It can be used to divide two sections of a wall or it can be used on its own as a freestanding molding, either horizontally or vertically.

Baseboard
Like a wooden baseboard, a ceramic one is intended to protect the bottom of the wall from damp mops and scratches. Some baseboards can be ordered with fully glazed top edges if no tile is to be placed over them.

Bolection
A molding, usually large and bulging, that can be used to surround a mirror or a fireplace opening when no mantel shelf is to be incorporated into the design.

Chinoiserie
A decorative style popularized in the late eighteenth century. Thomas Chippendale was England's greatest exponent of the style, but it was the French who coined the name and expanded its influence throughout the Western world.

Corbel
A small projection on a wall or a bracket that might support a shelf.

Cornice
Any decorative projection that derives from the ceiling and extends down onto the wall.

Corona
The projecting molding of a cornice.

Crown Molding
This, like a cornice, is meant to interface between a ceiling and a wall. Usually, however, it does so at an angle and most often will be curved in its section view.

Cyma
This word, literally translated, means "wave." The front surface of the Cyma Crown is wavy.

Dado
A molding that continues around the room and forms a chair rail or caps a section of wainscoting.

Fluting
Vertical grooves or flutes, usually with a concave profile, most commonly found running up the face of columns or pilasters and door casings.

Frieze
The flat middle section of a cornice, either plain or decorated.

Guilloche
A pattern resembling interlacing ribbons, generally linear in form.

Pilaster
A flat column attached to the wall.

Plinth
Decorative blocks on which columns or pilasters sit.

Rosette
A decorative element that can represent a flower or be as simple as a series of concentric circles forming a button.

Scotia
A deeply concave molding.

Sill
A projecting slab or molding at the bottom of a window or doorway.

Swag
Also known as a festoon or garland, a swag is a group of flowers or a drape that is gathered up and allowed to hang in a downward curve from buttons or supports at either end.

Torus
A large convex molding.

index

get wet

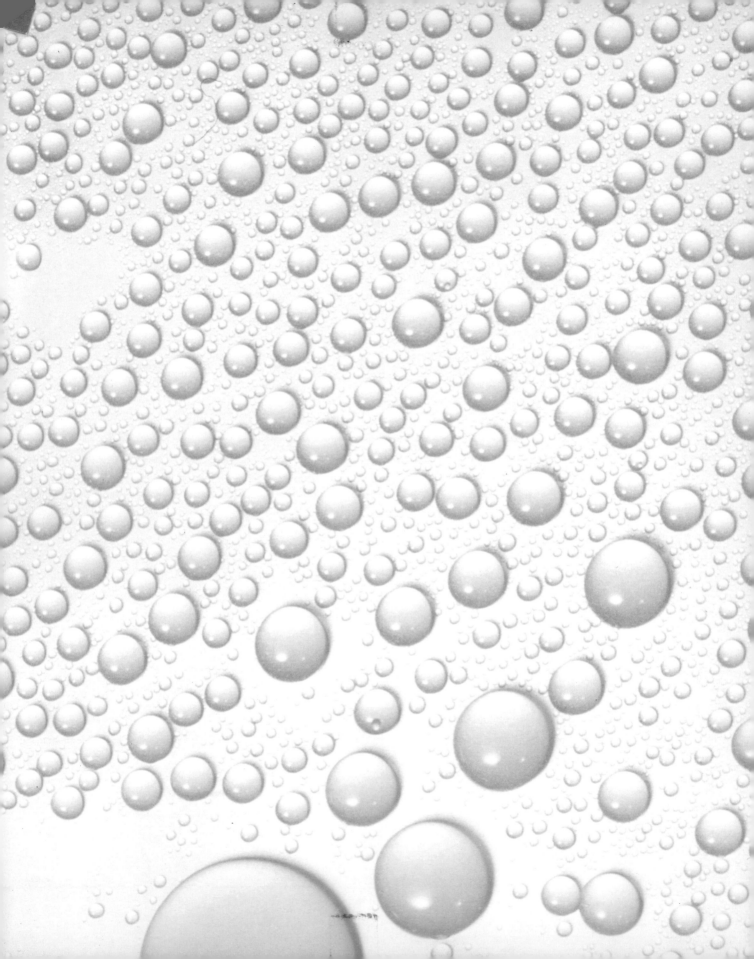